Symbols of Transformation in Dreams

Symbols of Transformation in Dreams

JEAN DALBY CLIFT
and WALLACE B. CLIFT

CROSSROAD • NEW YORK

1987
The Crossroad Publishing Company
370 Lexington Avenue, New York, N.Y. 10017

Library of Congress Cataloging in Publication Data

Clift, Jean Dalby.
  Symbols of transformation in dreams.
  Bibliography: p. 151
  Includes index.
  1. Dreams.   2. Symbolism.   I. Clift, Wallace B.
II Title.
BF1078.C55   1984   154.6'34   84-15557
ISBN 0-8245-0727-4

To
Anne, Lucy, and Bruce
our best friends

Learn as much as you can about symbolism; then forget it all when you are analyzing a dream.

—*C.G. Jung*

We and God have business with each other; and in opening ourselves to his influence our deepest destiny is fulfilled.

—*William James*

Contents

Preface

This book grew out of seminars and lectures we have given to various groups. From those experiences, particularly focused for us in a tour of Australia in 1983, we became convinced that many people engaged in a spiritual journey were interested in learning how dreams could enrich and guide their growth.

We have retained something of the informal mode of those oral presentations. Personal experiences and dreams are used to illustrate how insight can be gleaned from dreams. Where the illustrative material comes from our own lives, we have said so. Where the material comes from others, we have, of course, used only dreams and personal associations which the dreamers have specifically granted us permission to use, though the interpretations are usually our own. We have disguised their names and identities, but we here express our gratitude to all those who have so graciously shared their dreams.

It is our hope that this personal material will not only enliven the explanation of dream theory, but will also be of general help in understanding the process of working with dreams. It is with this hope that we have freely used many personal aspects of our own journeys.

Though we refer to some other theorists, our basic psychological position comes from the ideas of C. G. Jung, whose work we began to study in the early sixties. For us his insights into the meaning of life and of dreams have been personally transforming. Jung gave us not only a language with which to understand our spiritual journey in the Christian tradition, but with his teaching on dreams and their meaning, gave us an additional tool for making the decisions required on a spiritual journey.

Part I

The Language of Dreams

Dreams

Everyone dreams. Not everyone remembers dreams. Some people say they have never remembered a dream and doubt that they ever dream. Sleep researchers, however, say that everyone dreams each night whether the dreams are remembered or not. Furthermore, the research conducted by psychologists in sleep laboratories indicates that dreaming is necessary not only for psychic health but physical health as well. Dreams are apparently an essential part of the human experience.

The reality and importance of dreams have not been questioned in most cultures throughout human history. Dreams have been a primary basis for the belief in a psychic or spiritual realm that interpenetrates the physical world. The Australian aborigine spoke of the time of beginnings as the Dream Time, when things were different—before the arrival of the Europeans with their exclusive focus on physical reality. In Navaho religion dreams had much to do with disease and curing and were sometimes understood as a means of communicating with a spiritual realm. The approach to dreams was related to the belief in sympathetic magic; thus dreams of rain, corn and flowers were seen as good and dreams of drought were bad.[1]

Dreams have been a source of guidance not only for the individual but sometimes for a whole tribe or clan. In his travels in East Africa during the 1920s C. G. Jung found that the tribes he visited made the same distinction he did as a psychiatrist between "big dreams" and ordinary dreams. "Big dreams" moved beyond the purely personal material, often being concerned with the welfare of the whole tribe. Once he was told by a tribal informant, Jung said, that they did not

3

have "big dreams" so much anymore because now they had the colonial governor who gave directions for the tribe!

In the shamanic traditions of North America and central Asia dreams and visions were a recognized feature of a shaman's "call" to be a shaman. The historian of religions Mircea Eliade says, "It is in dreams that the pure sacred life is entered and direct relations with the gods, spirits, and ancestral souls are re-established. It is always in dreams that historical time is abolished and the mythical time regained—which allows the future shaman to witness the beginnings of the world and hence to become contemporary not only with the cosmogony but also with the primordial mythical revelations."[2] *Black Elk Speaks* is a good example of the story of such an experience.[3]

Revelation of divine truth through dreams was a generally accepted idea in Greek religion.[4] Visits were made to the temple of Asklepios at Epidauros for the purpose of healing; dreams and visions while sleeping in the inner temple were the means for meeting the divine healing power halfway.[5] Some dreams influenced historical decisions. Xenophon dreamed that lightning, with a great thunder, struck his home so that it appeared quite bathed in light. He explained the light immediately as the salvation that comes from Zeus, but it was also for him the sign of royal power, and the dream induced him to take on the leadership of the Greeks.[6]

The Judeo-Christian tradition also viewed dreams as significant. The Bible presupposes a psychic or spiritual world that interpenetrates the physical world. Modern Western civilization had not given the idea of psychic reality much credence until the quite separate developments of microphysics and depth psychology in the twentieth century. As a result of ignoring psychic reality, a lot of the material in the Bible has been ignored. In those churches and synagogues that insist on their clergy getting the same education that other professional people get, it has not been fashionable to talk about visions, dreams, or angels or any other suggestion of a spiritual reality.

The Scriptures were written over a period of nearly a thousand years of human history. They reflect varying understandings of the world and give a picture of the best "science" of their day. One does not need to advocate a literal reading of all the Bible, certainly not of its "science," in order to appreciate the accuracy of its portrayal of human life and experience. One assumption that lasted throughout that thousand years and on into the late Middle Ages was that a spiritual world impinged on the physical world. That was, of course, a view shared with the rest of the world's cultures. In recent years, the books of Morton Kelsey and John A. Sanford have called attention to how much of the Bible deals with this spiritual realm.

In the view of the Bible, angels, visions, and dreams are all part of the same reality. We might mention briefly a few examples. The patriarchs Abraham and Jacob were guided in most of their important decisions by dreams and visions. Both the Joseph of ancient Israel and the Joseph of the New Testament found the understanding of dreams to be of life-saving importance. The psalmist of ancient Israel probably had dreams in mind when he said, "I will bless the Lord who gives me counsel; my heart teaches me night after night." In the Rabbinical tradition, the Talmud says that dreams which are not interpreted are like letters which have not been opened.

The scholastic theologian of the thirteenth century, St. Thomas Aquinas, is called the "angelic doctor," and he did have an interest in angels and their reality. He described an angel as a thought that thinks itself. Many have probably had such an experience but did not think of it in such a personified way as an angel whispering in the ear, even if they knew the word angel meant "messenger." Spontaneous thoughts may be helpful, and they may be destructive. Probably most people have recognized "temptations"—thoughts about doing something they did not want to do or did not think was "right." In the picturesque language of the Bible, these are "fallen angels." Some of the messengers serve God, and some of the messengers are in rebellion against God.

Today, depth psychology has made it "respectable" to talk about dreams and waking visions and spontaneous thoughts. Jung wrote, "We could well point to the idea of psychic reality as the most important achievement of modern psychology if it were recognized as such. It seems to me only a question of time for this idea to be generally accepted."[7] The West, as Jung said, took physical matter for its prime authority and with that exclusive focus has given the world the benefits of modern technology, but the price for that development has been a neglect of the spiritual or psychic aspect of human existence. Perhaps even more than the depth psychologists, it is the science fiction and fantasy writers who have recovered an appreciation of the fact that to be human is to have both a body and a spirit.

In this century, microphysics, as it moved deeper into the physical world, has also discovered some non-physical aspects of reality. Subatomic particles, or rather, "energy charges," seem to be affected by whether they are being observed. Psychic reality (by whatever name) is getting recognized once again. We are suggesting, of course, that what we might call the spiritual world and the psychic world are part of the same reality.

This is not to say that we are suggesting a reversion to all the details of the worldview of the Bible or other earlier cultures, but it does mean that one need not dismiss some of the experiences of early peoples as simply "untrue" or as ignorant superstition. Rather, one can begin to understand some of the reported experiences in a new way, as "really" happening, even though one may doubt in some instances that a physical reality is being described. Another way of saying this is: the "supernatural" has become natural.

The recovery of an appreciation of dreams as part of human experience and therefore worthy of study also means that exploration can begin of the extent and of the ways in which dreams may provide some guidance or data for making the choices that must be made in life. One of the difficulties today in accepting dreams as providing additional data for making decisions is that most popular thinking about dreams stems from the understanding of Sigmund Freud. Freud discovered a basic truth about dreams: they give a picture of the psyche as it is. With his medical background, Freud was looking for clues as to what was *wrong* with the psyche so that he might find a basis for cure. Nineteenth-century science has been characterized as a "search for origins." Certainly that was Freud's approach. However, a picture of the psyche "as it is" also has within it the seeds for potential development, the possibilities with respect to the future. That is what Jung came to see: that dreams, as well as other unconscious material, should not only be viewed "reductively," as Freud did, but that they also provided clues for future development.

In Freud's theory there are irrational wishes and feelings that are unconscious and want to be expressed, but they are "censored" by an internal "censor." The function of a dream, in Freud's theory, is to preserve sleep, so the irrational wishes are disguised to deceive the censor. Freud viewed dreams as he did neurotic symptoms—namely, as a compromise between the repressed forces of the id and the repressing force of the censoring superego. Thus Freud's assumption is that the main characteristic of dream language is the process of disguise and distortion. The purpose of a symbol, in this view, is to disguise and distort. Dreams become a kind of secret code which must be deciphered. Symbolic language for the classical Freudian is confined within a narrow framework: it is understood as expressing only primitive instinctual desires—not any other kinds of feelings. In this view the vast majority of symbols are disguises for the many forms of the sexual drive. Present experiences trigger dreams in Freud's view, but their intensity and energy come from a childhood experience. Freud's theories have been modified in most current psychological practice, but they have permeated popular understanding.

Jung did not disagree with Freud's approach so far as it went, but he found it too limited. Jung felt that the energy of the psyche did not stem solely from the sexual drive, important as that was. Like the ego psychologists of today, Jung felt there were "independent ego energies." For its various thrusts into life the psyche was not dependent upon "capturing" the energy of the sexual drive through a process of sublimation, as Freud had taught.

In Jung's approach you take the dream for just what it says. A pencil *is* a pencil; if the male sex organ is the subject matter, then that is what appears in the dream (which it certainly does at times). Dreams can express the worst or the best in the dreamer. For Jung, there is no "censor" at work. Dreams may also be revelations of unconscious wisdom, transcending the individual. These are the kinds of dreams Jung's East African friends called "big dreams."

The humanistic psychologies of today, both religious and secular (or theistic and non-theistic), generally all assume that there is a potential for wholeness and that one reaches the goal of life through stages of development. Erik Erikson has suggested eight stages in life's journey. Abraham Maslow used the term "self-actualization" to describe the goal of the developmental process. Jung's term for the developmental process in the adult part of life is "path of individuation." Even St. Paul, in the New Testament, spoke of what was appropriate as a child and what was appropriate as an adult. Those psychologists who work with dreams generally assume that dreams are related to where the dreamer is in the developmental process of life. Dreams sometimes give signals of the moments in life when some transformation is called for, and these moments are the focus of this book.

Dreams are as varied as the people who dream them. Every dream is an experience in and of itself, an inner experience. Like an outer experience the dream may refer to the situation of the dreamer at the moment, or the period in the dreamer's life (the last several months or years), or it may move far beyond to the eternal or timeless realm. Western civilization has rediscovered the dream, and psychologists have found ways to help understand dreams. Dreams affect the person, however, whether understood, remembered, or forgotten. Dreams may leave one depressed the next morning or, on the contrary, bounding with energy.

It is our personal belief that dreams prepare the dreamer for the activities of the next day—with the psychic energy to strike out on new endeavors or carry through with something previously undertaken. We think this is true whether the dream is consciously noted or not. The advantage to trying to understand the picture of the psychic situation as the dream presents it is that the dream gives additional data upon which to base conscious choices. Paths of action not seen before may be recognized as possible. Understanding dreams is not essential for life, but they can enrich life and increase the possibility of making wise choices.

•2

The Unconscious

Dreams are products of the unconscious. One may well dream about some conscious worry or something that has grabbed one's psychic energy during the previous day, but what the dream does with it is not a product of consciousness. Although not always acknowledged, Jung's understanding of the way dreams function in the psyche is the basis of most approaches to dreams today. The relationship of the ego (defined as the center of consciousness) to the unconscious is the arena in which dream interpretation takes place in Jung's theory. Thus an examination of Jung's ideas about the unconscious is needed before proceeding to look at the symbolic language of dreams and the specific ways in which one may go about trying to understand them.

Jung was born in Switzerland in 1875, finished medical school in 1900, and went into the very new field of psychiatry. He developed what is called the "assocation test," by which hidden configurations of meaning can be discerned in the psyche. Jung called these configurations or emotionally charged patterns of meaning *complexes*. His investigation of the unconscious led him into a friendship with Freud, which blossomed very quickly after they met. The association lasted for six or seven years but ultimately resulted in a sharp break, each going his own way in the exploration of the unconscious. One area of disagreement was that Jung felt the sex drive was very important, but not the only determining factor or source of psychic energy as Freud insisted. Earlier, another associate of Freud's, Alfred Adler, had broken with him also. Adler felt the chief source or influence on character development was a struggle for power. Adler and his associates introduced into our language such ideas as sibling rivalry and inferiority and superiority complexes.

Jung felt both the sex instinct and the power drive were major factors in human development, but they did not account for all of his patients' problems. In his view, it was limiting to say Freud or Adler or Jung; rather, he urged that we say Freud *and* Adler *and* Jung—an inclusive perspective on the psyche. He found that his older patients also had a need for *meaning*. Worthwhile values and purposes are as necessary for life as the sex and power drives. Viktor Frankl, the contemporary Austrian psychiatrist, came to a similar conclusion, as is reflected in his system of "logotheraphy" or "meaning" therapy.

Jung outlined his differences with Freud, as he saw them, in a lexicon article in 1951: he did not think Freud's sexual theory of neurosis and schizophrenia was justified by experience; he thought the concept of the unconscious needed to be broadened beyond its definition as the product of repression; and he thought the personalistic, merely instinctual theory of the unconscious was too limited, as was the corollary wish-fulfillment theory of dreams.[1]

Very early Jung began to develop what he called a "constructive" understanding of dreams. His approach analyzes but does not reduce to some general principle such as "striving for power" (Adler) or "sexuality" (Freud). Jung's constructive approach breaks dreams or other unconscious systems of human expression down into typical components, which he found by the comparative analysis of thousands of dreams. Jung also discovered that countless typical formations in individual material showed obvious analogies with mythological formations, which aided in bringing the meaning of the dream to light. The perception of individualized systems of order which seemed to serve a teleological function in the psyche led Jung to doubt that the contents of the unconscious were "nothing but" repressed complexes. He thought Freud's reductive method simply did not do justice to the profusions of symbols produced.[2]

It was the discovery of repeated reversion to archaic forms of association found in schizophrenia that first gave Jung the idea of an unconscious of a different nature from Freud's theory. It was:

> ... an unconscious not consisting only of originally conscious contents that have got lost, but having a deeper layer of the same universal character as the mythological motifs which typify human fantasy in general. These motifs are not *invented* so much as

discovered; they are typical forms that appear spontaneously all over the world, independently of tradition, in myths, fairy-tales, fantasies, dreams, visions, and the delusional systems of the insane.[3]

Freud's theory of sexuality also implies, of course, common universal motifs, which he referred to as "archaic remnants," but Freud was not interested in pursuing these remnants further. Jung's theory simply broadens the scope and nature of human motifs and instinctual psychic factors far beyond the sexual. Freud's devotion to the "sexual dogma," as he himself called it, precluded further mutual work after Jung's "desertion" of that dogma.

The study of comparative anatomy from Jung's medical training became for him an analogy which led him to his theories of what is sometimes called the "objective psyche," and more often, the "collective unconscious." He pointed out that just as the human body shows a common anatomy over and above all racial differences, the human psyche also possesses a common "substratum" transcending all differences in culture and consciousness. This substratum is the *collective unconscious,* common to all humankind, and consisting of "latent predispositions towards identical reactions."[4]

To test out his theories of the collective unconscious, Jung traveled to Africa and to the United States to study African and American blacks and native American Indians, as well as reading and studying extensively in a wide range of historical, anthropological, and philosophical subjects. He became convinced by all these studies that the mind of a newborn child was not a *tabula rasa,* or clean slate.[5]

Thus Jung's developed theory of the unconscious includes two "layers": the collective unconscious (described above) and the personal unconscious. The latter contains recognizable material of a definitely personal origin, such as forgotten or repressed contents, but also creative contents as well, of which the individual had not been aware.

While acknowledging that the personal unconscious was, *in part,* the product of repression, in Jung's view the unconscious as a whole was the creative matrix out of which consciousness developed. Since the unconscious was in part seen as collective, he rejected the theory of its merely instinctual nature developed out of personal, individual experiences. Instead of Freud's wish-fulfillment theory of dreams, Jung emphasized, as we will show, the compensatory function of the unconscious processes and their developmental function. In Jung's view

the unconscious is largely composed of hitherto undeveloped, unconscious portions of the personality which, as he said, "strive for integration
in the wholeness of the individual."⁶

Jung called the collective patterns and figures from the collective
unconscious *archetypes,* using an expression he found in St. Augustine.
An archetype in Jungian theory is a *typos* or imprint, a definite grouping
of an archaic character containing mythological motifs. As the collective
unconscious is the repository of human experience and at the same
time the prior condition of this experience and has taken aeons to
form, certain features or dominants have crystallized out in the course
of time. These patterns are what Jung called archetypes. They are
restored to life, Jung found, by the primitive, analogical mode of
thinking peculiar to dreams. Jung thought these archetypes were
inherited thought-patterns, and he felt that the instincts and archetypes
were so close to one another analogically that "there is good reason
for supposing that the archetypes are the unconscious images of the
instincts themselves, in other words, that they are *patterns of instinctual
behavior.*"⁷

Jung also repeatedly denied the accusation of detractors that his
theory of archetypes meant that the *specific* content of ideas was
inherited. One denial of this (among innumerable others) outlines the
difference:

> Again and again I encounter the mistaken notion that an archetype
> is determined in regard to its content, in other words that it is a
> kind of unconscious idea (if such an expression be admissible). It
> is necessary to point out once more that archetypes are not
> determined as regards their content, but only as regards their form
> and then only to a very limited degree.⁸

Observation of the times when archetypes tended to appear led Jung
to see that archetypal material appeared in the dreams of "normal
people" when they were in life situations that were threatening, such
as moments of mortal danger, before or after accidents, severe illnesses
or operations, or when psychic problems were developing which might
give their life a catastrophic turn, or when a change in a previous
attitude was being forced upon them by some new circumstance.⁹ Jung
perceived that the reason for the appearances of archetypal images into
consciousness at such times was connected with the inward movement
of their psychic energy. Since such movements only occur at moments

when a new orientation and a new adaptation are necessary, Jung said that the constellated archetype is always the primordial image of the need of the moment. In other words, "moments of transformation," as we have called them in this book, will frequently be signaled by archetypal motifs appearing in the dreams.

Although it may seem that the changing situations of life are infinitely various, Jung said their possible number never exceeded certain natural limits. Human experiences fall into more or less typical patterns that repeat themselves over and over again. The archetypal structure of the unconscious, in other words, corresponds to the average run of events. "When therefore," Jung said, "a distressing situation arises, the corresponding archetype will be constellated in the unconscious."[10]

Jung said archetypes manifest themselves not only in images but as emotions. Thus, it is "a piece of life, an image connected with the living individual by the bridge of emotion." It is "living matter." It is the emotion which represents the *value* of the archetypal event. Jung saw a great danger in applying a purely rational analysis in the interpretation of an archetypal moment, for such a thinking-type intellectual process does not include the intense feeling value. This feeling factor forms the link between the psychic events and their meaning.[11] In Jung's experience the appearance of an archetypal image indicates the need for some major change. If the conscious mind can succeed in interpreting the constellated archetype in a meaningful and appropriate manner, then a transformation can take place.

Jung spoke of *symbols* as transformers of psychic energy.[12] Only through symbolic language can the feeling factor and the emotional content, about which Jung spoke, be communicated with sufficient force to bring to consciousness the nature of the choices available. The transformation thus involves both *experiencing* the emotion carried by the image and *understanding* the symbolic significance of the image. The understanding contains the meaning of the image, and the emotion contains the energy to bring about the needed change or transformation.

Symbolic Language

The twentieth century has brought the recognition of the planetary nature of the human spirit. World War II forced into consciousness the awareness of the interdependence of all peoples on the planet. Politicians and statesmen began to speak of "one world." As we have said, much earlier in the century Jung had recognized a "oneness" in the archetypal expressions of the collective unconscious, whose patterns and motifs are expressed in symbolic language.

Symbolic language is a language in which inner experience, feelings, and thoughts are expressed *as if* they were sensory experiences or events in the outer world. Symbolic language is different from the language ordinarily spoken in daily life. It has a different logic. Time and space, for example, are *not* the ruling categories that they are in outer life. Rather, the ruling categories are intensity and association. The psychotherapist Erich Fromm says it is the one universal language which the human race has developed—the same for all cultures and throughout history. His book on dreams in the early fifties was entitled *The Forgotten Language,* for so it was in the West until the coming of depth psychology.

Symbolic language is not only the language of dreams, but it is also the language of myths and fairly tales. It is the most basic way in which people are able to grasp an idea. From his observation of the psyche, it was Freud's surmise that picture language precedes thinking in words. A striking discovery about the psyche's production of motifs is described in *Roots of Renewal in Myth and Madness,* where the Jungian analyst John Weir Perry has indicated that symbolic language is to be found in the psychotic delusions of schizophrenics. Perry found that in its attempt to rebuild the ego as the center of consciousness and recover a relationship of the individual to his or her world, the psyche produced kingship motifs like those in the world's mythology. Understood symbolically, the psychotic delusions could be seen as attempts of the psyche to strengthen the ego. In Jungian theory the ego is defined as the center of consciousness, that is, of one's awareness of oneself as an individual.

The materialistic worldview of Western culture has hampered the development of a sensitivity to symbolic language, even though it is the one universal human language. This is perhaps another reason dreams have not been accorded the attention they received in other cultures. Jung said symbols "are images of contents which for the most part transcend consciousness."[1] He said people still have to discover that, though partly or completely unknown, symbols are *real* and seek to express some meaning, and he cautioned that it was not only possible but absolutely necessary to come to terms with them.

Jung made a sharp distinction between signs and symbols. The theologian Paul Tillich made exactly the same distinction, and Tillich's language is particularly helpful in explicating Jung's understanding. Tillich said signs point to something; they point to another reality. Symbols, like signs, also point to another reality, but in addition they *participate* in the reality to which they point. A symbol *makes present* the other reality. For example, this is a way of understanding the function of sacraments in the Christian tradition.

There are always two aspects of a symbol: the concrete, this-world aspect (that of which one is conscious) and the other reality to which it not only points, but which it makes present (the aspect that is unconscious). In other words, a symbol bridges two realities. In personal work, the symbol is a bridge between consciousness and the unconscious. In religious symbols, the bridging is between this world and the other world. Jung found that the symbols of their religious tradition were no longer "alive" for many people. That had been his personal experience and was the experience of many people who came to him for help. The symbols had become signs, no longer mediating the presence of another reality; they lacked personal association and intensity. This, of course, is not surprising in view of the exclusive focus on material reality of western European culture, as previously mentioned.

Pictures or stories are often needed to talk about feelings, moods, values, emotions. This is the nature of symbolic language. Stories communicate and stories make use of symbolic language. For example, love is a primary value and experience in human history. How do you communicate what love is? You cannot say it is green and weighs three pounds; you have to tell a story of what love is like.

In the same way, how do you describe a mood? You can use descriptive words, but a story or a dream picture of a particular experience may capture the mood far more precisely. Artists often speak the symbolic language, making use of the categories of intensity and association. In symbolic language the world outside is a symbol of the world inside.

In the world of literature, writers have described the relationship of signs and symbols in almost exactly the same way as depth psychologists and theologians. Usually contrasting their approach to symbols to the use mathematicians make of the word "symbol," literary critics describe a symbol not as existing for its own sake, like a dollar sign, but instead as pointing to a meaning beyond itself. Symbols are viewed functionally, seeming to be part of what they stand for. Even when the symbol used denotes a physical, limited thing, it carries enlarging connotations. The meaning is usually somewhat ambiguous, but still it carries emotional power and suggests multiple meanings. It intimates a larger reality. Poets and other writers have had the same difficulty with the modern age which theologians encounter because so many traditional or conventional symbols have lost the power to move people in the same way. Symbols in dreams, religious tradition, and literature all share the quality of presenting insights into an unseen world. The meaning is real, yet elusive.

Many critics divide symbols into two categories: conventional symbols and symbols which particular writers breathe life into by the skill of their literary creations. A conventional symbol might be the country's flag, which at times arouses strong emotional reactions. During the late 1960s when the nation was divided about foreign policy, some of the citizens put the flag on their bumper stickers, perhaps with an added admonition such as "America, Love It Or Leave It." With equal emotion another segment spoke symbolically of their view of the country's political positions by sewing flags on the seat of their blue jeans. Both were using the conventional symbol of the flag to mean something more than itself—to point to the values for which it stood; they were interpreting the way the country could serve those values differently.

In the same period of time, poet and song writer Pete Seeger took a river in Louisiana called the "Big Muddy" and used it to make a political statement about America's escalating involvement in Vietnam. Whether one agrees with Seeger's political assessment or not, it is clear that he uses this symbol in such a way that one knows exactly what he means. The Captain of a platoon on maneuvers instructs the men to wade the Big Muddy, though his Sergeant tells him the river is too deep and the men will drown. In the story of the poem, the Captain starts to lead the men, drowns, and the Sergeant turns them back around. The emotional force of the poem occurs in the repeated lines, "Waist deep in the Big Muddy/And the Big Fool says to push on." The poet has made the river live as a symbol.

Erich Fromm suggests another helpful differentiation of kinds of symbols. In Fromm's division there are conventional symbols, accidental symbols and universal symbols. Conventional symbols are really signs as defined above. That is, there is only one meaning, as with the signs used in mathematics or the pictures on road signs. Such conventional symbols direct a specific action, as the plus sign says to add two numbers or an arrow says to turn left.

Accidental symbols derive from personal experience or the experience of a local group. For a few years after President Kennedy's assassination, "Dallas" was for many a symbol of horror because he was killed in that city. A decade or so later, Dallas would raise for many the values and stereotypes of the television show of that name (for some, still another kind of symbol of horror). Accidental symbols that are personal to an individual often occur in dreams, and, as we will discuss, personal association with the symbols in dreams is the first step in understanding what the dream might be portraying. These kinds of personal symbols would not, of course, appear in myths and folk literature, though on a larger scale, some associations peculiar to the experience of a particular culture would be reflected in the folk literature of that group.

Universal symbols derive from the common experience of humankind. There is an intrinsic relationship between the symbol and that which it represents. For example, fire has some characteristics that are common to human experience all around the planet and throughout the human encounter with fire. It is "alive," dancing, changing continuously, and yet constant. It has power and energy; it gives light. It burns and destroys and can be painful, and yet it cleanses. Fire transforms matter from one form to another, to smoke and ashes.

Water is another example of a universal symbol. It is a part of common human experience. It also presents a picture of the blending of change and constancy and is alive with energy. It can also be slow, quiet and steady. It can be destructive and is also an essential of human life. One can see part of the way into water, but not into its depths, so it suggests the experience of the unconscious. It is a method of cleansing and, not surprisingly, is symbolic of cleansing in many of the world's religions.

Body language is a universal symbolic language. Hearts beat faster with emotion, and poets have made use of this knowledge to portray emotion. Blood rushes to the head in a fury or in embarrassment. Though universal symbols have these common associations, they may be modified in different cultures. For example, the role of the sun is different in the Arctic and in tropical regions. Water has a different function and a different appreciation in the rain forests and in the desert and so may symbolize a different experience.

Jung cautions that a true symbol cannot be merely invented:

> There was never a genius who sat down with his pen or brush and said: "Now I am going to invent a symbol." No one can take a more or less rational thought, reached as a logical conclusion or deliberately chosen, and then disguise it as a "symbolic" phantasmagoria. No matter how fantastic the trappings may look, it would still be a *sign* hinting at a conscious thought, and not a symbol. A sign is always less than the thing it points to, and a symbol is always more than we can understand at first sight. Therefore we never stop at the sign but go on to the goal it indicates; but we remain with the symbol because it promises more than it reveals.[2]

This is one way of expressing why genuine symbols cannot be precisely "interpreted" by any one single meaning. Jung says they are always "ambiguous, full of half-glimpsed meanings, and in the last resort inexhaustible"; their essential point, however, is "their *manifold meaning, their almost limitless wealth of reference, which makes any unilateral formulation impossible.*"[3]

Jung pointed to the danger in reducing a symbol to some specified, rational explanation. This danger occurs with the increase in human consciousness. As the individual becomes more conscious, he or she is increasingly threatened with isolation, which, as Jung says, is the "*sine qua non* of conscious differentiation." The greater this threat of isolation, the more it is compensated by the appearance of collective and archetypal symbols which tie one in to that which is common to all. Naturally, this works for the individual only so long as the symbols have not lost their numinosity and thrilling power. Once this has occurred, they can never be replaced by anything rational. Jung saw this as the trap in which the medieval alchemists and Freud were caught: they could never get at the meaning of their symbols because they were caught in some reduction, which insisted that the symbols had a specific meaning, which in fact was less than the symbols themselves. When the symbols themselves are allowed to live, their meaning can continue, and Jung says they have strong power to do so:

> Luckily for us, symbols mean very much more than can be known at first glance. Their meaning resides in the fact that they compensate an unadapted attitude of consciousness, an attitude that does not fulfill its purpose, and that they would enable it to do this if they were understood. But it becomes impossible to interpret their meaning if they are reduced to something else.[4]

Probably no aspect of Jung's approach to dreams is more important than this caution to let the dream symbols continue to live. Many times a dreamer arrives at some understanding of a dream's significance very near the date when the dream was dreamed. However, if the symbols themselves remain alive in the dreamer's memory, that significance may continue to be enhanced. We have had the experience of understanding some aspects of a symbol at the time of the dream, but realizing other aspects as much as fifteen years later! Such continuing enrichment cannot occur if one reduces the dream symbols to some specific concrete equivalent. This balance is an acquired skill for many— to try to understand the symbol, yet not to concretize it. We have found Jung's suggestions for how to approach dreams to be of help in walking this tightrope.

•4

Approaching the Dream

Dreams not recorded immediately upon waking may soon be forgotten. If it has not been recorded, only occasionally will a dream continue to haunt the dreamer or pop back into memory. Usually getting a dream recorded requires a quite disciplined effort. Recording materials need to be set out the night before. It is "as if" such a ritual assures the unconscious that communication may be possible. No matter how sleepy one is or how trivial a dream fragment seems, it needs to be written down. As a few words are put down, more come along. Someone has compared getting anything from the unconscious to fishing—you have to keep pulling in the line even though you don't know what you have caught, if indeed anything.

You record all the facts you can: setting, people, time, ages of the people, furniture in the building, kind of building or landscape description if outside, feeling tone (pleasant or frightening or anxious), words heard, thoughts that came during the dream—all that can be remembered about the dream. Many people find it helpful to give the dream a title after the details are recorded, summing up the general theme or focusing on a major image. Dating the dream is also important, for insights may be discovered by correlating the dream with events or attitudes present in one's life at the time.

As noted in chapter two, Jung's understanding of the psyche is that the unconscious contains not only repressed material but also creative possibilities for development. Another way to speak of this would be to say that the unconscious contents when brought to consciousness can enhance the clarity of conscious choices; there is more accurate information on which to base those choices. In this sense, you can understand the unconscious as being, in effect, "on your side." As we have suggested, dreams have a constructive role to play in psychic functioning, whether understood or not. However, if one can grasp something of the meaning or possibility or the unadapted attitude which the dream is holding up, then there is a wider base upon which to make conscious decisions.

Jung regarded the dream as a kind of "snapshot" of the psyche, providing a description in symbolic language, of the current psychic situation. "Dreams," he said, "are the natural reaction of the self-regulating psychic system."[1] This understanding of the *compensatory* quality of dreams is the principal key to Jung's approach to dreams. When one has an attitude or view which is too one-sided or exaggerated, the dream may show a picture of an exaggerated or one-sided stance in the opposite direction. If you are afraid of something, you may find yourself being chased in the dream; if you are ignoring something, you may get hit over the head with it in the dream. What is consciously viewed as too high is brought low in the dream or vice versa. Dreams may also show some fact of which one is consciously unaware; they may portray blind spots. Another common compensation a dream may suggest is the result which occurs when one hangs onto an attitude whch may once have been appropriate, but which has now outlived its usefulness.

Jung himself gives a clear example of this compensatory function in a dream he had about a patient of his. He says that the analysis was not going well, and he felt that he was not getting at the correct interpretation of his patient's dreams. He decided to speak to her about this, and the night before he planned to speak, he had this dream:

> I was walking down a highway through a valley in late-afternoon sunlight. To my right was a steep hill. At its top stood a castle, and on the highest tower there was a woman sitting on a kind of balustrade. In order to see her properly, I had to bend my head far back. I awoke with a crick in the back of my neck. Even in the dream I had recognized the woman as my patient.[2]

Jung realized immediately that if in the dream he had to look up so high to see the patient, he had probably been looking down on her. The distortion was so severe that it was a "pain in the neck." When he told the patient of his dream and his interpretation, he says the treatment once more moved forward.

In this example, Jung decided that the dream showed him that he had fallen into a one-sided stance which was blocking him from seeing his patient "properly," even as the dream language suggested. In such dreams, one is likely to speak of the dream as "telling me what to do," but notice that the dream does not give Jung a direct "message" that prescribes his future behavior. It simply tells him, by the compensatory imagery, "how it is"—what his conscious attitude is. He made the decision, based on that information, that he would modify that conscious attitude, but he might just as well have decided that he did not choose to modify it. He simply had more information than before the dream on which to base his choice.

There are many shadings and gradations of the forcefulness of compensatory imagery. Apparently, if the conscious attitude is extreme, the compensating dream image will be equally extreme; whereas if the attitude is only slightly inadequate, the dream imagery will be much closer to the outer perception—complementary to consciousness. This is one way in which the dream manifests the level of intensity.

Not all dreams are as clear as this dream of Jung's, of course; and people sometimes wonder why it is so difficult to understand them. Part of the reason seems to be precisely because the unconscious really is unconscious. It consists of that of which one is not aware. It takes great courage to face some of the insights which dreams suggest. The personal unconscious does consist, in part, of matters that have been repressed or not admitted—as Jung's attitude toward his patient demonstrates; but there is material in the unconscious that sometimes appears in dreams which has never been a part of personal life experience. There are "dragons to be slain" which were never a part of the world in which one grew up. The existence of the collective unconscious means that individual consciousness "is not immune to predetermining influences."[3] Quite apart from the obvious and unavoidable influences exerted upon it by the environment, individual consciousness is subject to the inherited presuppositions of the collective unconscious. In Jung's view, as we have said, the unconscious is the matrix out of which consciousness develops, and while there is a natural "thrust into life" that helps to promote and develop consciousness, there is also a kind of "pull" back into the comfort of the "womb." That explained, Jung felt, the extraordinary *resistance* which the conscious puts up against the unconscious. "It is not a question here of resistance to sexuality," Jung said, "but of something far more general—the instinctive fear of losing one's freedom of consciousness and of succumbing to the automatisms of the unconscious psyche."[4]

This difficulty of apprehending the meaning of dreams is sometimes overcome by the fact that if you miss the meaning the first time around, the psyche may present you with more and more insistent pictures until you do finally pay attention. It even seems as if the first time or so, the dream images are relatively mild, but if you miss the point, they may become darker, more troubled, finally even violent, as if to make the point even to the dreamer who runs.

This is only one of the reasons that Jung preferred to analyze a series of dreams instead of just one dream. Not only does the repeated motif suggest that the matter of the dream is important, but if you keep a dream journal and can read over a whole series of dreams, you can often discern a pattern. The same theme may be repeated, or a particular dream figure may recur repeatedly, but in slightly different situations. Thus you may discover implications or a progression or development that would not have been recognized in any single dream. A dream is only a part of the "psychic tissue," which is continuous. Jung stressed that "we have no reason to think that there is any gap in the processes of nature."[5] The continuity in a motif can be especially instructive, as we will illustrate with some dream series in later chapters.

Jung also observed that the figures in dreams sometimes can be interpreted objectively and sometimes subjectively.[6] (Sometimes they can even enlighten one both objectively and subjectively.) When dream figures are interpreted objectively, they represent themselves. If you dream of your neighbor, for example, the dream may be calling to your attention something about your relationship with your neighbor. Jung's dream of his patient is such an objective dream. When he worked with the dream, he reached a new, hitherto unconscious, awareness of his devaluing attitude toward her. In objective interpretation, one simply views the people and objects in the dream as representing what they are in the outer world.

To look at a dream on the subjective level, one takes each part of the dream as an aspect of oneself. For example, a husband's dream about his wife would be looked at as involving an encounter with his feminine side. If you dream of a tiger, you ask yourself where your tiger within may be lurking. If you have a dream, as many people do, of "discovering" a new wing to the house, then one possible meaning of the dream which should be considered is that there is another part of the dreamer's life which has not been discovered, possibly a new potential worth exploring. The clues to the nature of that new potential can be found partly in the details in the dream (what rooms and furniture did the wing contain? what could one do in the wing? how did it feel to be there?) and partly in the current personal circumstances in the dreamer's life. As with all dreams, the whole truth of the psyche is not contained in any dream, but they do give clues to the parts not seen.

A puzzling question is: how do you know whether a dream is objective or subjective? Jung felt that the great majority of dreams are to be interpreted subjectively, with the figures all representing parts of the dreamer. We have found that it is helpful to approach the dream at first as if it were objective. If the dream figure is someone with whom you are in current contact or who has current psychic significance for you, then you ask: what does the dream suggest about the relationship? Sometimes you will feel that immediate "click" which Jung evidently felt in the dream about his patient. You realize with a shock that you have unconsciously held an attitude toward the dream figure of which you were unaware. Even if the click of recognition is not immediate, thoughtful attention to the issues raised in the dream may give you a dawning new awareness, and you will know that you have learned something by the objective examination of the dream story.

When, however, after honest examination, you can make no sense of the dream on the objective level, or when the dream gives you no information on the objective level which you did not have before, then you turn to the subjective. Sometimes you are inclined to go to the subjective level at once, when the figure is someone with whom you have never had or do not now have any relationship. Then you begin to ask yourself questions such as: What part of me could that be? When do I behave that way? Where can I find that in me? Sometimes the feeling tone of the dream can be the most important clue to this discovery process. Some dreams make sense on both the objective and subjective levels; something new can be learned in both ways.

Freud used the method he called "free association" to pursue the significance of the symbols in dreams. He would begin with the original image and ask the patient to follow the train of thought which the image suggested until the "hidden" sexual image was reached for interpretation. This can be diagramed in a continuous straight line, and it is the last image in the line which is interpreted; this method is consistent with Freud's theory that the dream was a disguise for a thought which the unconscious dared not produce.

Though Jung agreed that significant information could be obtained from free association of the patient, he felt, as we have said, that the dream image itself was of more importance. To explore the dream's meaning, he taught a method of association he called "amplification." Each symbol or aspect of the dream is amplified, first, by the dreamer's associations with the symbol. By this Jung meant any spontaneous thoughts, feelings, sensations, intuitions, or memories that come to mind concerning any given person or image in the dream or in response to the dream as a whole. In themselves, these personal associations may suggest a significance for the dream. The dream may even remind the dreamer of something that seems totally unrelated, but that, too, is helpful for the exploration of the meaning. This personal context should be explored before any other approach to the dream is made. Jung spoke of this as *personal amplification*.

Sometimes it is difficult to make these personal associations. We have found it helpful to write down, perhaps in a list, all of our associations with a person or image that we have dreamed about. This can be helpful whether the image is someone you are in regular contact with or someone you have never met. It can be the most useful, perhaps, when the image is bizarre or shameful. John Sanford has suggested a helpful game to play if it is difficult to associate with a dream symbol; he suggests one pretend one is trying to explain the symbol to someone who has just landed from Mars and asks: what is that?

One woman we know had a dream about Elliott Gould, and when she was asked, "Who is Elliott Gould?" she replied that she knew him only through parts he had played in films. As she thought of her general ideas about him, she realized that her main association was that he usually played the part of someone who acted as if he were less capable and much dumber than he actually was. With that association, she could then ask herself: do I sometimes act as if I am less capable and much dumber than I actually am? Her rueful laughter was her answer, and then "Elliott Gould" became a handy way to catch herself in that rather destructive pretend-game she had played for years, largely unaware that she was doing so. In this way, her own association with her dream figure gave her a continuing, living symbol to tease herself with; when she caught herself behaving that way, she could inwardly chide, "Oh, come on, Elliott."

After the dreamer's personal associations with the symbols have been traced, the dream may become quite clear, as we said; but sometimes, additional depth and meaning can be reached through the approach which Jung called *general amplification*. The analogical method of association is made not only with the dreamer's personal associations, but also with mythology, history, folklore, anthropology, zoology, or any other branch of learning from which some insight into the way the image has been understood may be found. The symbols the psyche produces are molded by personal experience, but they are grounded in archetypes of the collective unconscious. Much of the work of Jung's followers has been addressed to the study of myths, fairy tales, religious symbolism, and the natural analogies which have presented themselves to people throughout human history. As is frequently pointed out, a person who wishes to explore dreams from a Jungian perspective needs to be acquainted with all the learning of the historical and imaginative world. Clues to dreams can be found in remarkable places.

The use of general amplification has validity, in Jung's view, because "we are not simply of today"; as he stated in a filmed interview with the BBC, "we are of an immense age." Just as the physical body has a history, so the psychic aspect of being human has a history. The human body contains a whole museum of organs, with a long evolutionary history behind them, and, so Jung said, one should expect the psyche to be organized in a similar way rather than to be a product without a history. By "history" Jung did not refer only to a personal story, that is, the development of the mind through conscious tradition (language, etc.); but rather, he referred to the formation of the collective unconscious through the long evolutionary history of humankind. Just "as the morphologist needs the science of comparative anatomy, so the psychologist," Jung said, "cannot do without a 'comparative anatomy of the psyche.'"[7] The depth psychologist thus needs a wide acquaintance with mythology, religious traditions, folk tales, and the great literature of the centuries, as much as a wide acquaintance with dreams. Both are areas of study in Jungian training.

No matter how much amplification, general and personal, is done with reference to a dream image, in the end attention should always return to the dream image itself. A diagram of this work might be a wheel, with the image at the center and the various associations which amplify the image as spokes around the hub; and it is always to the central image that the dreamer returns. With the gathered knowledge of the associations, some of which may not be helpful in understanding the image, the dream image as it was dreamed originally is lived with and allowed to speak to the dreamer without any attempt to reduce it to some theory or explanation. These images, for one thing, have more power to continue living than the abstraction of their reduced explanation. In the example above, it is more powerful to be able to say, "Oh, Elliott, cut it out," than it is to assure yourself that you are actually more capable than you feel at the moment. The former approach has the living quality of a relation with a person; the latter is more likely to feel like a judgment that enervates rather than energizes. When the image in a dream connects with a primordial archetypal image from the collective unconscious, the dreamer can become connected with transcendent powers of transformation.

When dreams deal with details which are like ordinary life—with houses, cars, buses, and so on—they are probably dealing with issues close to daily life, which have been called "daily housecleaning" dreams. When, on the other hand, there are fantastic elements, mysterious worlds or creatures, or settings far from the present, they may well be dealing with deeper issues from the archetypal levels of the psyche.

Dreams that occur around special days may have special significance. The "initial dream" when one begins to work with a dream interpreter or a dream group often gives clues for the issues that one needs to pay attention to. New Year dreams or dreams around anniversaries also carry this special kind of importance. Many people like to watch to see what dream they have on their birthday. Even the sound of the date of one's birthday gives pleasure to the birthday person, so it is not surprising that special dreams sometimes come from the psyche on birthdays.

One helpful way to think about amplifying figures in a dream has to do with the age of the dream figure. One may dream, for example, that one is about eight years old in a dream, or there may be another eight-year-old person in a dream. A good approach to this is to ask if the dream might be associated with something that happened when the dreamer was eight years old or else with something that happened eight years ago. Some activity which began eight years ago may be personified by the dream figure.

Some dream interpreters view dreams of oneself at an earlier age as an unhealthy regression, as if one were behaving like an eight-year-old. It may be so, of course, but it also may be true that one needs to re-experience or rework something which occurred at that age. Jung did not view all regression as unhealthy. Regression may be in the "service of the ego," of course, which would mean that one was behaving with inappropriate immaturity.

On the other hand, regression can be in the "service of the Self," in which case it is conducive to growth or restorative to health. If the energy of life is not caught in a rigid stasis, regression is just as normal a polarity to progression as sleeping is to waking. If growth and understanding are moving freely, the movement backward in regression will eventually turn into a movement forward in progression. The particular dream experience needs to be carefully examined to determine what needs to become conscious.

An approach to amplification through the methods of literature study has also proved helpful to us; the literary approach to symbolic language is a simple way to learn how to think analogically. We discuss some aspects of this literary critical process in the next two chapters.

•5

Amplification by Poetic Figures

Clues for amplifying dream symbols can be found in the detailed examination literary critics give to the symbols in poetry. The way a poet communicates emotions or insights to the reader is comparable to the way the unconscious tries to communicate the unsuspected nuances in the psyche. The experts of literature have practical and concrete suggestions for finding the meaning of symbols through the study of the *figures* of speech.

Most students learned the basic vocabulary of poetic interpretation at some point in their early schooling, but a review may be helpful, beginning with some definitions. An "image" in poetry is something concrete which communicates directly through the reader's senses. The concreteness is important because the image must carry directly from the writer to the reader in a manner which abstractions cannot do.

Concrete nouns make good images. For example, if the writer speaks, as Emily Dickinson frequently does, about a "bee," the reader sees exactly the same thing the writer does. Details may vary, but essentially the same group of characteristics become present to each reader. Readers experience the same sensory picture Dickinson saw when she wrote. The sensory details include not only visual but the other sense impressions as well; some of the richer images appeal to a number of the senses at once. Even in the simple "bee," one not only sees but hears with the poet. Because they also communicate clear sensory details, many action verbs also are good images. When one hears the word "skipping," one experiences the same kind of concrete image.

A major means by which poetry functions is to compare a concrete image by analogy with something abstract or otherwise incommunicable by language from one mind to another. A simile is a comparison between two essentially unlike things using the words "like," "as," or "than." A metaphor uses the same kind of figurative comparison without the comparative words, implying the comparison instead of stating it. The two things being compared are called the "terms" of the simile or metaphor. There are many forms of metaphor—explicit, implied, extended—but the essence of the symbolic process is that the concrete is used to make present to the reader something which is not otherwise so easily perceived.

When Jean taught college freshman English, she used a famous Robert Burns poem to illustrate the process by which these comparisons communicate. In the poem Burns says, "O, my luve's like a red, red rose / That's newly sprung in June." He wants to tell readers how he feels about his love, whom they do not know, so he begins with a simile which compares her to an image which they can experience with him—a rose. Jean would ask the students in the class what qualities a rose had that Burns might want to compare to his love, and the students, being freshmen and usually determinedly anti-sentimental, would supply such answers as: it wilts; it has thorns. We think there may be something in those answers, but there is also even more in the qualities one more frequently associates with roses: it is beautiful, it smells sweet, it is ever unfolding (especially one that's newly sprung), it is fresh, cultivated, living—the associations can go on and on.

Notice also that each detail is important in stating what kind of lady love he has. His love is like a "red, red rose"—there is a striking, vibrant quality to her. Imagine, for instance, how different she would sound if he had said she was like a snow white rose or a pale pink rose. Those would be possible loves, but quite different women.

Another sense perception, that of hearing, is added when Burns next says, "O, my luve is like the melodie / That's sweetly played in tune." Readers then perceive not only the beauties of music with all its associations, but the order, the sweetness, and the sense that she stays in the memory like a tune one cannot forget.

Readers do not have to go through this process in detail, though— they experience a quick perception in their feeling response even before they go through any analysis of the concrete terms. The poet has carried them with him into his psychological experience of his love. They believe Burns's speaker when he spends the next three stanzas of the poem promising devotion to her because the force of his imagery has captured for them the force of his caring.

The same experience happens to dreamers in many of their dreams—even if they have not analyzed the dream's meaning, their emotional attention can be captured with an intensity which forces their energy into certain paths. How many times people say that they woke feeling exhilarated and able to accomplish some task by the force of a dream; or perhaps they woke feeling depressed and without energy because of some dream that pulled them down. They have these emotions in response to dreams, just as they have them in response to some poems. Yet, as the poem is enhanced by analyzing and understanding the images, so the dream can become more useful to their growth if they understand and analyze its meaning for them. Then the felt emotion can become part of their conscious awareness in detailed ways.

What happens when an image is understood is that a bridge has been made between the evoked emotions and conscious knowledge. Another powerful example to illustrate this bridging aspect is in the Langston Hughes poem "Harlem."

> *What happens to a dream deferred?*
>
> Does it dry up
> like a raisin in the sun?
> Or fester like a sore—
> And then run?
> Does it stink like rotten meat?
> Or crust and sugar over
> like a syrupy sweet?
>
> Maybe it just sags
> like a heavy load
>
> *Or does it explode?*

Here Hughes takes one term—the abstract term which is not an image—"a dream deferred," and he compares it to a series of images in order to help the reader feel with him what happens when anyone's hopes and dreams cannot come to fruition. Though the title of the poem and the fact that Hughes himself is a black American show that he writes specifically about the deferred hopes of urban black people, the poem has universal application to the dreams of all.

Notice what happens to the emotions in the successive encounter with this series of images. Raisins made from shrivelled grapes are sweet and nourishing, but when one thinks of a human being shrivelling like a raisin, one shares the sense of limitation with regret and sorrow. This feeling becomes sicker with the repulsive image of the running sore, turning to nausea when the next image suggests the spoiled smell of food gone bad.

Then Hughes almost plays with the reader by turning from "spoiled meat" to "syrupy sweet"—the exact rhyme and the alliteration driving home the comparison. By the fact that they are next to each other and are related in sound so precisely, these two images are connected. If, for example, one thinks of the syrupy sweetness of the kind of fawning obsequiousness which was frequently necessary for survival in a slave culture (and which has become a term of disdain when still practiced by blacks known to other blacks as "Uncle Toms"), one connects such sweetness to rotten meat, suspects it, and rejects it. The sweetness is tainted by proximity to the stink.

The stress on this point is important because dreams frequently play just this way. One image or scene in a dream is placed next to another which seems unrelated, until one focuses on the way in which the proximity of the two affects the emotions. Then their very proximity teaches something of a dual vision. The reader is able to see the relationship between seemingly unrelated parts of unperceived mixed attitudes. This is an example of the way some dreams "walk around" an idea or attitude to give different perspectives on it.

The last two images in the poem probably have a similar connection to each other. At first in the image after the stanza break, there is a little emotional relief from the tension between sweet and stink. Readers, too, can sag under the heavy load and feel a (deceptive) sense of resting. Even in that respite, though, the nature of the image in the action verb "sag" is worrisome. There is a tiredness in this sagging response to the heavy load, and, again, the weariness of the overworked slave is present. Then Hughes blasts readers with the last, italicized image: explode. Again there is a connection of the rhyme of "explode" and "load," in this case by identical sound. The italics join the first and last lines of the poem, suggesting, or we might even say, threatening the reader with the awareness that the poem's last question may indeed be the answer to the first question.

This is bridge building at its best, as the reader is carried powerfully to new awarenesses of the strong emotions present in the poet. In addition, this poem shares other qualities with dreams—with dreams while sleeping, that is. It asks questions. Many dreams do precisely that. By the very asking of the questions, the poem prods the reader to find answers other than those listed, none of which is satisfactory. Just so, many a dream presents the dreamer with possibilities so shocking that he or she is prodded to conscious action in order to forestall the threatened picture. This poem, like so many dreams, works by giving an awareness of danger; then, if one has the will to do so, one can make other conscious choices in full cognizance of the danger of not doing so. One can take on personal responsibility more fully. Thus the images in the dream build bridges between consciousness and unconsciousness so that choices can be made with expanded knowledge. The dream images, when their significance is grasped, become not only the image but the vehicle by which conscious action can be carried out.

Another common figure in dreams and poetry is personification, which occurs when human traits or attitudes are placed on something not human. This kind of metaphor always has a human being as one of the terms of the metaphor and something not human as the other. Most people probably encountered as children the tree "whose hungry mouth is pressed/Against the earth's sweet flowing breast," and the "naughty sun" who stayed abed one day so the child missed seeing his companion, the shadow. Personification is one of the earliest kinds of metaphor or bridge builder encountered. Yet it can also be subtle, as in Tennyson's fragment "The Eagle."

> He clasps the crag with crooked hands;
> Close to the sun in lonely lands,
> Ringed with the azure world, he stands.
>
> The wrinkled sea beneath him crawls;
> He watches from his mountain walls,
> And like a thunderbolt he falls.

Eagles do not have "hands," so there is here an interplay of animal and human characteristics which help one share the experience of the eagle. In its authentic description, the poem moves through the eagle's experience of commanding height, isolation, clear observation, and, at the last, the power of all nature after its prey. The accuracy of the experience puts readers in touch with the eagle within them, just as dreams of animals and even inanimate figures put one in touch with those parts of oneself—one's own trees, flowers, suns, moons, eagles, tigers, dogs, kittens. The nature of the image reveals its qualities, just as the personification of the poet does.

Dreams even pun, not only playing on two possible meanings in words that sound alike, but frequently branching out into the dual meanings in common sayings. A dream might show an unmusical dreamer playing a "fiddle" to suggest in the colloquial pun that the dreamer was "fiddling" around. Jungian analyst James Hall's patients have many insights while standing in hallways as a pun on his last name, as we have seen many dreams that take place near "cliffs." A dream may act out quite literally that the dreamer "can't stomach something" or that some person or action "turns the dreamer's stomach." In dreams, people find themselves "stiff-necked," "on a high horse," or looking around behind something to see "what lies behind it." The possibilities are as endless as human language in one of the dream's most playful ways of communicating.

This is only one of the kinds of allusions that poems and dreams make to material outside their own context. Indirect references to historical, biblical, mythological, or literary material are common in dreams. Anyone who works with dreams soon feels a sense of awe at the immensity of material available in the human psyche. It was, of course, just such dreams which first led Jung to his discovery of the collective unconscious, where the entire experience of human development becomes a resource for each person's psyche. Many of the allusions are unknown to the dreamer, and aid from outside resources helps in understanding them.

Two other figures used by many poems and dreams are overstatement and understatement, sometimes called hyperbole and litotes. Such images are a way of seeing the operation of what Jung calls the compensatory function of dreams—when the dreamer is over-balanced in one direction, the dream image will be over-balanced in the other. The extremity of the pictured image is a good clue to how extreme the conscious has become; some dreams contain very slight "corrections," others are radical.

Poetry also uses these figures to create special effects. When Burns promises his red, red rose that he will love her till all the seas go dry, the rocks melt with the sun and the very hourglass of life itself has run out, the overstatement creates an elaborate statement of his promise, but in the tone of this poem, one believes that he believes his promise.

The reader has quite a different response to similar assertions in Andrew Marvell's "To His Coy Mistress."

> Had we but World enough, and Time,
> This coyness Lady were no crime.
> .... I would
> Love you ten years before the Flood:
> And you should if you please refuse
> Till the Conversion of the Jews.

From the title of the poem, from the irony evident in his attempt to seduce his lady, one forms an opinion of their relationship quite different from the hyperbolic nature of his claims. In this case, a compensatory effect is experienced from the overstatement.

Likewise, understatement can be effective in producing the opposite response in the reader. When Wordsworth mourns the death of the maid, Lucy, who "dwelt among untrodden ways," one feels his loss the more because he understates it, "oh, / The difference to me!" When Emily Dickinson speaks of dying in "I heard a fly buzz when I died," the small buzz of the fly in the face of the hugeness of death takes the reader with the poet into emotion more than would a direct statement of the awfulness of the experience. These figures have a compensatory effect.

Yet apparent understatement is precisely what many poets use to give an exact snapshot of the image as it really is, as when Frost's speaker stops to watch the woods fill up with snow or takes the road "less travelled by, / And that has made all the difference." In such understated images, the poet nevertheless is not suggesting a compensatory reaction so much as he is placing his life in as exact a context as possible so that if one experiences the same feeling with him, it is because one has shared a similar view of life.

The clue which suggests whether the figure is used for a compensatory function or as a psychic snapshot of just the way it is, is the context— the tone, the other images used, the discernible theme. Such clues can also be helpful in thinking about whether or not dreams suggest compensation or direct pictures of how it is—one of the more troublesome puzzles in dream interpretation.

Amplification by Poetic Structure

Another helpful area of literary study is the examination of the *structure* of the poem to see what can be learned about its meaning. There are some traditional patterns in which poems have been constructed for centuries and some newer modern developments; all of these patterns also occur in actual dreams.

A common structure is the narrative form which tells a story from the beginning, through the middle, to the end. There are poems of this type from simple ballads to book-length epics. Dreams also sometimes tell a story, sometimes simple straightforward stories. Some mornings on awaking, though, it feels as if one has been through an epic to rival Homer or Milton. Narrative progression customarily includes the original setting, the arising of a conflict, a climax, and a denouement or conclusion in which there is a resolution. In dreams, one frequently wakes with the sense that part of this narrative action has been lost to memory, but it is surprising how many times a complete narrative emerges even from a remembered fragment. It is usually helpful to observe carefully how the narrative progresses—including the changes in mood or feeling in different parts of the dream. Details of the narrative form can illuminate even apparently straightforward narrative dreams.

For instance, a dream may tell in narrative form a story which is similar to something which has actually happened. Invariably, however, there will be some change from the actual event. Then one can focus on the change to see wherein the dream suggests something different as a hint to change the perspective or attitude to the event. A dream may be using the narrative form to correct or to suggest some unrecognized factors, so that one's understanding can be enlarged.

Beyond this simplest experience, the dream has endless complexities. Maybe the dream is in narrative form so that the dreamer's life can be explored as a story, or the form of the story may show that the dreamer has been living as if life were a fairy tale. Perhaps the dream may warn against continuing a present attitude, lest the dreamer in fact be headed for acting out a Lady Macbeth or Othello or Willie Loman. Perhaps the dream may show the potentiality that one is like the autocratic father in *Life with Father* or has the potentiality to become Joan of Arc or even a cartoon cat-and-mouse character. Whatever the narrative presented, it is important to remember that dreams are not necessary destiny. No one is an automaton; we all have freedom of choice. Everyone needs to know more about any hidden dangers and potentialities in order to make good choices, in little matters and in large. Thinking about dreams as if they were stories may indicate ways in which life really is open-ended.

The narrative structure may reveal an inner drama of which one is unaware. Emily Dickinson in her poem #747 recounts such an inner process:

> It dropped so low—in my Regard—
> I heard it hit the Ground—
> And go to pieces on the Stones
> At bottom of my Mind—
>
> Yet blamed the Fate that flung it—*less*
> Than I denounced Myself,
> For entertaining Plated Wares
> Upon my Silver Shelf—

The movement of the poem shows the emotional progress of the speaker in the poem with precision. Something—an idea, a friend's integrity, perhaps—disappointed her so strongly that it felt to her as if a dish had dropped and broken in her mind. The first stanza gives this powerful emotion in images familiar to the homemaker. The second shows how she worked out the emotions toward a new understanding of her complicity in the disappointment. She was tempted to blame Fate at first, but then saw that she, too, deserved some blame because she had put silver plate on the shelf reserved for sterling. With the value put onto silver plated wares today, it may be hard to appreciate the days in which "plate" was a term of opprobrium, but the reader can follow her thinking to realize that she overvalued "it," though she should have known better.

One can follow this process even with no idea at all what the specific situation in the speaker's life was; the "it" remains an unknown referent. Many narrative dreams are like this. An outsider can look at a dream and describe the process or movement in the narrative, but until the dreamer adds the personal amplification, the outsider cannot make a connection between the dream and whatever life situation the dream relates to. With personal amplification, however, the narrative structure enables the dreamer to compare any current life situation with the movements and feelings of the dream; thus the narrative form may lead directly to new insights.

Another form of poem and dream is organized by logic. For example, some are organized by cause and effect—almost as if the poem or dream says: if A occurs, then B follows. Some cause-and-effect dreams are also in narrative form, but others seem to present scenes which may have no obvious relation to each other, until the first scene is viewed as a possible "cause" of the "effect" in the second.

A related form of poem follows a logical order or progression, though not necessarily that of cause and effect. The logic may be in several patterns. It may begin with a general observation and then focus in on details, or it may begin with a series of details and arrive at a general view. There may be a kind of expository progression which develops clarity as the exposition proceeds, so that there is more knowledge at the end than there was at the beginning. There may even be a logical argument in which one side is presented and then the other. This can be done by contrast, almost as if the dream first presented one side and then said, "On the other hand . . . ." The logic may come from a series of different pictures of the same theme, with each picture adding depth and breadth to one's perception of the theme.

A deceptively simple poem which is organized by logic is Robert Frost's poem "Fire and Ice."

> Some say the world will end in fire,
> Some say in ice.
> From what I've tasted of desire
> I hold with those who favor fire.
> But if it had to perish twice,

> I think I know enough of hate
> To say that for destruction ice
> Is also great
> And would suffice.

This poem presents "arguments" for one side and then the other. The language is straightforward; the tone is quiet, understanding the enormity of the subject matter. The subject matter itself operates both on the stated level of world destruction and on the inner level of psychological destruction of an individual, with the use of the personal words "desire" and "hate."

The effect of the poem on the reader is achieved from the quiet logic, the almost casual way in which the horror of destruction is observed—the focus being not on *if* the world will be destroyed, or even *when*, but assuming that, then *how*. Such a poem can jerk readers to attention, so that they begin to be aware of how important it is to forestall the destruction, both socially and personally.

A similar "argument" can occur in a dream as can the other logical structures listed above. The knowledge that all these logical forms are possible certainly does not explain which is applicable to a given dream. However, a consideration of the various possibilities can bring that sudden click which provides the dreamer with an insight otherwise easily missed.

Jean had a dream at the beginning of her analytical work in Zurich which presents a set of rather humorous pictures of her attitudes and fears about the Jung Institute. She recorded the dream as follows:

> There was a scene in a large hospital with several floors where some kind of fest was to take place. So they kept making people go in other directions so they could get ready for it. There was someone there whose language I tried to translate. Was it a church?
>
> Later I was at home and a watchmaker was redoing the house, and I did not like the way he was doing it. But I was somewhat afraid of him, so I kept trying to make it turn out the way I wanted it without a direct conflict with him. There was something about a bench which he wanted horizontal in one room. I wanted it vertical.

The Jung Institute is probably suggested by the "large hospital with several floors"—a place devoted to healing. The dream presents a droll view of the investigation of the unconscious—making people go in other directions so they can be ready for the party! And, indeed, it is like learning to translate another language to become familiar with the terminology of psychology.

An even funnier image is raised by the question whether the hospital is a church. True believers of any school of thought do tend to take on various habits, rituals, and creeds as if they were devotees in a church, and Jungian psychology is no exception, despite Jung's own aversion to creeds and dogma.

The second paragraph of the dream moves it closer to "home" for the dreamer and suggests that a watchmaker (one of the most famous crafts for the Swiss and probably referring to Jean's analyst at the time, who was a native Swiss) is re-doing Jean's house in a way she doesn't like. She does not say so, though, but only tries to manipulate it the way she wants it to go without admitting it openly. Dreams play such funny tricks; the dream itself, when taken to the analyst, told him precisely what Jean thought she was so cleverly keeping from him.

The last two sentences define symbolically the difference in opinion between analyst and analysand: the analyst wants her to have a "horizontal" place to sit, and she wants a "vertical." This refers, certainly, to Jean's determination to understand the relationship of the insights of psychology and Christianity in a way which did not lose the "vertical" relation to God. Jean was at that time suspicious that the Jungians would try to disprove God to her, and the dream raises that issue in the second paragraph.

This dream contains a series of different pictures which elaborate a single theme. Interpreting the dream's form as a whole shows the expository clarity which can give the dreamer more knowledge at the end than she had at the beginning. She can see precise images of her own psychological position.

One of the most elusive kind of dreams is one which might be called a "T. S. Eliot dream," after the twentieth-century poet who had such a profound effect upon modern poetry and criticism. Eliot was one of many contemporary poets who were dissatisfied with the old structures of poetry and sought new ones. This kind of search is one that always goes on in the history of literature, but the twentieth century has produced some of the most radical breaks with tradition. Beginning with the freedom from traditional meter and rhyme, contemporary poetry has attempted to express the variety and complexity of today's world. Some critics say it only succeeds in being obscure.

Eliot spoke of the organization of poetry around what he called an "objective correlative." He said there was no longer a shared worldview, so that a poet could no longer assume that any particular symbol system which the poet used would be understood by the readers. Therefore the poet was constrained to try to find images which objectively correlated to the emotions and thoughts the poet wanted to portray, and those images had to evoke the correlative feelings so clearly that the poem itself created a symbol system which communicated between poet and reader.

Some images have this capability, such as Burns's red, red rose, so that readers can imagine what kind of love Burns had by the nature of the image he used. However, no longer are most contemporary poems using these images in a straightforward, descriptive way. Instead, the meanings are evoked in a number of different ways. There are leaps from thought to thought without any transition between them. Apparently unrelated images are placed next to one another, though their moods are so at variance as to seem ludicrous at first. Language is mingled in ways which would have horrified previous centuries—colloquial with formal, intellectual with the bizarre. The poems are full of surprises and weird contrasts and comparisons.

In short, the poems act a lot like many dreams, which seem to have no central theme, but instead to be a jumble of unrelated symbols and bizarrely unconnected events. It seems singularly appropriate that such poetic forms arose at the same time that the depth psychologists were paying increasing attention to dreams. Bringing Eliot's poetic techniques and insights to bear upon the interpretation of dreams leads one to see that some dreams do not speak by logic at all, but rather by creating emotional responses through their rapid, evidently unrelated images, and especially by the fact that these are juxtaposed with one another in discordant, even nervous patterns. One can begin to see that a dream which leaps about irrationally may be trying to express disintegration by its form, as Eliot did in such poems as *The Waste Land*.

In his first published poem, "The Love Song of J. Alfred Prufrock," Eliot creates a clear picture of the state of mind of the speaker of the poem with no logic or descriptive detail of him at all—the poem is a dramatic monologue. This effect is achieved by such lines as the sophisticated refrain, "In the room the women come and go / Talking of Michelangelo." In contrast are such images as these:

> And indeed there will be time
> To wonder, "Do I dare?" and, "Do I dare?"

Time to turn back and descend the stair,
With a bald spot in the middle of my hair—

Would it have been worth while
To have bitten off the matter with a smile,
To have squeezed the universe into a ball
To roll it toward some overwhelming question,
To say, "I am Lazarus, come from the dead,
Come back to tell you all, I shall tell you all"—
If one, settling a pillow by her head,
    Should say: "That is not what I meant at all;
    That is not it, at all."

I grow old. . . . I grow old. . . .
I shall wear the bottoms of my trousers rolled.

Shall I part my hair behind? Do I dare to eat a
    peach?
I shall wear white flannel trousers, and walk
    upon the beach.
I have heard the mermaids singing, each to
    each.

I do not think that they will sing to me.

Even these few excerpts take one inside the speaker, arousing whatever reactions of sympathy, pity, disdain, or impatience connect with one's responses to such a man.

In such a dream, with one disjointed scene following another, it can be helpful to think of it in terms of Eliot's poetic form. Then one looks for the objective feeling which is a correlative for each image or scene in the dream. When the dreamer has "felt into" each of the scenes, then he or she can turn attention to what is evoked by placing each scene beside the next and can thus draw closer to the psychic snapshot which the unconscious is presenting in the dream. The emotional content of the scenes or images carries the conceptual content of the dream. Modern films frequently use this same quick, disjointed form with one scene piled on another to elicit in the same way the emotional response from the viewer.

In a sense this *is* a logical structure. Such dreams, when understood as a series of objective correlatives, are in fact proceeding in logical progression—from idea to idea by cause and effect or by dramatic unfolding. The logical structure is not apparent on the surface, however, because it is hidden in the images and the feelings they evoke.

This hidden structure is one reason that such dreams become more available by the techniques of Gestalt therapy. When the dreamer acts out the various parts of the dream, the emotional content becomes presently apparent.

For example, take a dream with two apparently unrelated scenes:

> I dreamed I was seeing what looked like the ruin of a Greek Temple all by itself out in a deserted countryside. It was beautiful, even though it was just a ruin. There was a peace and stateliness in the whole atmosphere. It felt very quiet.
>
> Then suddenly, I was in a nightclub or something in some place like New York, and everyone was watching a go-go dancer gyrate at an ever increasing tempo to a loud rock band. The pitch of sound rose higher and higher till I woke up.

A Gestalt therapist might ask the dreamer to "become" the Greek temple, feeling all the mood and silence and peace of that scene. Then the dreamer might "be" in the nightclub, re-experiencing that scene—perhaps even as the go-go dancer herself. Then the dreamer might move back and forth between them, experiencing the change directly from one to the other and back again. Such a contrast would obviously be experienced as extreme. Then the dreamer would be ready to explore where such a conflict was currently present in her life. What present situation held such extremes of hidden emotions? When the conflict is thus brought into present awareness, the dreamer can begin to examine what can be done about the conflict.

Another helpful aspect of bringing such awareness to a lively consciousness is that the dream images are so vivid that they can continue to be used to interpret life experiences which come after the dream. In the example above, for instance, when the dreamer becomes conscious that the crescendo of life is approaching the breaking point as it did in the nightclub, the dreamer can consciously elect to call up the other resource from the Temple scene—can imaginatively "go" to the peace and serenity of the long-neglected Temple in order to be restored to serenity from her own inner depths. At the same time, the dreamer may be grievously misled if she does not stay aware of the go-go dancer within, who is also part of her and needs to be recognized and given space and air. Otherwise, the peaceful Temple may be a dead ruin without life. The two halves of the picture seem to be too extreme, too far from each other, and some kind of balanced choice is probably needed. In such a manner, the scenes from dreams can continue to inform one in living symbols of the ways in which one can understand and order one's life by conscious choice.

Part II

Some Motifs of Transformation

•7

Transformation

Life is change. Growth is natural. In all of life, whether in plants or animals, there are changes from one stage to another. So it is also with that form of life which human beings know personally. The human story, as many contemporary personality theorists see it, is a story that describes the process of change called "development," with different "tasks" required at different times in life.

In the beginning of human life, physical growth and change is the most obvious. Tremendous development is also taking place in the mind or spirit, the non-physical aspect of being human, but these changes are largely discernible only by the adoring parents. Many contemporary psychologists, in various ways, have described a pattern of development that is natural to the unfolding of the human psyche in the course of a lifetime. There are different developmental tasks that are appropriate to different stages of life, and many psychologists and psychiatrists have specialized in their attention to a particular stage in the life journey. There are child psychologists, vocational counselors, marriage and family counselors, and counselors for the terminally ill. Recently, more attention has been given to the problems of transformation at the time of the so-called mid-life crisis.

Freud can be credited with opening the door to the study of developmental stages in childhood. Freud himself dealt only with adult patients; but it was his observation, perhaps it could even be said to be his "discovery," that the adult was subject to influences from the unconscious that affected behavior. The unconscious was, for Freud, the repository of life experiences. In a sense, for him, the child was parent of the adult. He saw himself, it has been suggested, as the "great liberator"—a second Moses—for he wanted to set people free to consciously choose their behavior instead of being slaves to unconscious forces.

Building on Freud's theory of stages of development in childhood, Erik Erikson has delineated eight stages of development that extend from infancy to old age.[1] Erikson describes each stage as a "crisis" with two possibilities tugging at the individual. Erikson recognizes the interplay of the developing psyche with its environment, and consequently his schema is described as a psychosocial theory of human development. With the successful resolution of each conflict or crisis a new strength is developed. Erikson describes the successive stages as having a cogwheeling effect: the successful resolution of each stage is an aid to the successful resolution of the next stage. Without reviewing all eight stages, some examples might clarify Erikson's approach to the transformation processes called for in life. The crisis for infancy, the first stage, is between trust and mistrust; and the ethical value or strength to be achieved from a successful resolution of that experience is hope. Hope is the basic building block of life. It is what pulls one into life and the future. Erikson's seventh stage, adulthood, entails the choice between generativity and self-absorption. The strength to be developed here is care. For the eighth and last stage, the crisis faced by the older person is between integrity and disgust or despair. The strength to be developed here Erikson calls wisdom.

Transformation motifs are frequently found in dreams because life is a journey, with potential for growth and development as long as it lasts. As with any form of life, being true to the essence of one's individual being, to one's roots, is essential to development—and to having a sense of meaning in life. Jung found that, after the "roadblocks" thrown up by the circumstances of their lives had been cleared away, many of his patients were still not "at ease" with life. Their lives lacked meaning. They still lacked, as he said, what the living religions had always supplied to their followers: a sense of meaning, a sense of being related or connected to a larger reality than their own sense of being an individual ego. Contrary to the common Western approach of viewing healing as a violent treatment from outside, most cultures have tended to view healing as a kind of transformation.

What if the symbols of the religious traditions have become mere signs, as they have for so many today? The answer lay, Jung felt, in recovering an appreciation of the symbolic language that had always been present in human experience and by means of which the individual ego could be related to a "larger reality"—namely, through dreams.

Jung's theory of human development entails a "first half of life" and a "second half of life." He did not have in mind a necessarily specific number of years with respect to either "half," but spoke only in general terms. These developmental stages pointed to the kinds of transformation needed in the course of life.

The first half of life is devoted to getting established: acquiring the needed tools in school, finding a partner and making a home, and getting established in one's business or profession. The sex drive and the power drive are both primary concerns—one has to choose how one will live with them. Complexes or disturbances in these areas can lead to neurotic behavior patterns. Neuroses are, in Jung's view, improper displacements of psychic energy, and the symptoms that neuroses tend to produce in the first half of life are frequently characterized by a hesitancy to enter into these pursuits in the outer world. On the other hand, when the attitudes appropriate to that period are carried over into the second half of life, they then become inappropriate. Jung accounted for the problems so often associated with the middle years of life by the failure to make this shift in concerns and attitudes. The tasks are different at different stages of life.

In the second half of life, one has to come to terms with the inner world, just as one had to do with the outer world during the first half of life. As the first half entailed the making of many choices and going down one path instead of another, the second half entails a re-examination of the roads not taken in order to reclaim any values laid aside by the earlier choices. Perhaps at the later period these values hidden in the other roads can now find appropriate new life. This "other side" is buried in the unconscious, and raising that to consciousness results in a new sense of power. Such an experience has been described in the spiritual history of all great religious traditions as one of "rebirth" or renewal.

Jung's description of the process of transformation in life is comparable to Erikson's description of the stages of development. Both have a goal of wisdom. People have grown "wise" long before modern psychologists described how it was accomplished! Gordon Allport, the late Harvard psychology professor, once wrote:

Throughout the ages the riddle of individuality has been explored by the giants of literature. Tardily, the psychologist arrives on the scene (someone has said, two thousand years too late). To some humanists he looks like a conceited intruder. One critic complains that when psychology deals with human personality it says only what literature has always said but says it less artfully.[2]

Jung also concluded that the goals of the human developmental process must have been perceived or recognized, however dimly, long before the development of Western scientific approaches. Jung found in the world's myths, folk tales and fairy tales the same motifs that he found reflected in the developmental patterns of his patients.

Creation myths can be found in most, if not all, of the world's cultures. One of Jung's associates, Dr. Marie-Louise von Franz, asserts that, understood psychologically, they describe in pictorial language the experience of either the beginning of consciousness, or the coming to consciousness of a fragment of experience.[3] Hero myths could be said to be creation myths in microcosm, for they are stories about the task of creation within the individual. The individual may serve the whole society—that is often the case for important culture heroes, but the task is one the hero accomplishes within. The hero may have help, but ultimately an inward integration must take place. If the hero is able to follow through, then there is a new release of creative energy available. However, to be true to the whole task in the basic pattern of the hero story, this treasure of new creativity should also be available for others. The hero "brings back the treasure" to share with the tribe, the community, the world.

Incidentally, as we use the term, heroes may be either male or female. The usual connotation of the word "heroine" suggests a particular functional role. Heroines are not heroes of the feminine gender; they are people who are *rescued;* they are passive. Heroes are people who move out and accomplish something; they rescue or find the treasure. Because these connotations are so strong, we prefer to use "hero" in a gender-free way; we do not use "heroine" at all.

We also are not using "hero" in the sense of one who feels a demand to achieve and come out on top like an old western movie, nor are we talking about any particular culture's ideal hero, which tends to be a reflection of that culture's values. The archetypal hero pattern is rather a picture of the process of growth.

On the journey the hero becomes a different person. It is ultimately a story of *transformation* and growth. Sometimes the growth is in strength of a physical sort, but usually it is a growth in "wisdom." The hero returns home a wiser person, a more developed, a more humane person. This is what the hero has to give to the people or the tribe. To achieve this, the hero has had to undergo trials and hardships and do battle with all sorts of things. Only one who can overcome these "dragons" can attain the "treasure." Some heroes undergo a kind of death and rebirth experience. In the beginning of the journey, there may have been some pain in parting, a difficulty about leaving the home territory. The "foreign" is usually frightening. Afterward, the hero may be tempted to stay in the distant land, rather than undertake the difficult journey back home, with more possible dangers and trials.

The hero often has the experience of feeling that it is necessary to "abandon all" in order to undertake the journey, or may feel "abandoned by all." It is a lonely journey, with some friends and helpers along the way sometimes, but still a journey the hero undertakes alone. Transformation is always the experience of an individual. The individual, as Jung says, is the carrier of consciousness. The hero journey is a picture of the ego's escape from some unconsciousness by a conscious retrieving of some value hidden or lost. The return then presupposes the integration of that value, bringing it into daily living in conscious form. The hero *is* the one who, refusing to be swallowed in unconsciousness, makes the enormous effort to become more conscious.

The hero story in its myriad forms gives expression to the basic tasks of human development, and hero symbols appear in dreams when the ego needs strengthening. Sometimes the hero story may be dealing with tasks of the first half of life. They may be concerned with building an identity, establishing oneself as somebody in the world. This involves a "going out"—explorations, perhaps acquiring something or doing some task. The new experiences of young people become a part of who they are. These tasks of the first half of life have a *heroic* quality.

Then, too, in what Jung called "the second half of life," there are other tasks which should culminate in the finding of some meaning in the whole business of life. This entails also a "going out" from the ego position which has been established and encountering an "other"—a larger meaning than just that of the individual ego. One of the motifs here is *sacrifice,* a motif found in so many of the world's religions.

Understood psychologically, it is a sacrifice of the ego—the ego gives up something of itself in order to be in relationship with a larger meaning. In religious language, it is giving one's life to God.

The peculiar thing about this is that in making this sacrifice the individual discovers a truer and more vibrant individuality than ever before. This is the paradox of the Christian journey, and it is the "wisdom" which is acquired in all successful hero journeys concerned with the developmental tasks of the second half of life. Not surprisingly the world's great religions present stories that resonate with the hero journey, with the spiritual journey the soul must travel. Jung called the world's great religions the world's great psychotherapeutic symbol systems.

Jung understood the basic story of the evolution of life on the planet as one that entailed the gradual development of consciousness. He saw that the story of human history, or perhaps one could say, the goal of human development, as a story of ever-increasing consciousness. Each personal life journey will inevitably reflect or be a variation on the general basic human story. The more of which one is aware, the better basis one has for making choices. He hoped the "right" choices would be made—namely, ones that would serve life and not death, but his fundamental presupposition was that to be human is to have choices presented.

He further stressed that transformation, not sublimation, is the goal of human development. It has been pointed out that transformation postulates a change in the person instead of a mere adaptation of destructive drives to society's standards. As a result of the kind of transformation which Jung suggests, the drives would cease to be threatening and destructive and would be converted into helpful elements.[4]

The *path of individuation* is Jung's term for the psychological development in what he called the second half of life. His own experience and that of his patients led Jung to identify the archetypes of the developmental process: the *persona,* the *shadow,* the *anima* or *animus,* and the *Self.*

The archetypes of the developmental process are customarily presented in that order; however, any given individual life may require confronting and coming to terms with a particular developmental archetype before attention has been given to one usually or typically encountered earlier. Life may present a man with an *anima* problem that has to be dealt with before he has begun to achieve any integration of his *shadow*, for example. Not that the encounter with a particular archetype is ever "finished"—new, and also old aspects of the shadow, for example, will continue to be met throughout life. Jungian analyst and psychiatrist James Hall has written, "In the process of individuation there is no single creative or heroic act, but rather a succession of transformations over a lifetime, each straining and testing the ego anew—a series of what Neumann referred to as calvaries."[5]

Dreams often present clues about the current task with which the psyche is confronted. In the following chapters we present dreams which illustrate the archetypes of the developmental process. We also take up other motifs which have commonly appeared in the dreams and unconscious material of people at moments when some possibility of transformation is presented to them. By the examination of particular examples, we are not, of course, suggesting any universal pattern either of development or of interpretation. We are rather trying to illustrate by example methods by which one can begin to relate to the myriad symbols which the psyche presents.

In all of life, in nature, there are signals when a new development is about to take place. A few of these are obvious: a bud precedes the flower, the flower usually withers before the seed begins to be formed. Jung discovered that in the psyche there were also signals or indications of a transformation possibility. Often such a signal is even presented in the form of a crisis, as in Erikson's description. In his exploration of the unconscious, Jung found that dreams frequently presented images signaling those moments of transformation, those moments in life when the possibility of a new development is presented, a transformation which one can either go forward with or reject. Sometimes the images are in personified form, but the process itself may appear in what Jung called the *archetypes of transformation*.[6] The following chapters explore some transformation motifs and suggest ways of beginning to grasp their manifold meaning and of consciously responding to them.

•8

Persona

Jung used the term *persona* to characterize expression of the ego's archetypal drive toward adaptation to external reality and collectivity. The term comes from the masks that actors wore in ancient drama. It refers to the roles everyone plays in everyday life. Every individual needs a system of adaptation or way of meeting the world. One must necessarily hold oneself out in some way at each point in life. At the same time, there are usually expectations from the outer world: for example, ministers never misbehave, doctors know how to cure everything, nurses are always obedient, etc. Each profession tends to assume its own characteristic persona or way of accomplishing the adaptation. The persona each person wears is the adaptation made to these two realities: one's sense of personal identity on the one hand and a sense of what others are expecting on the other.

At first glance, for many, the idea of a persona sounds like something to be rejected. Today people feel that it is better to be honest and not wear a "mask." Jung was not against honesty—in fact, honesty is what an increase in awareness or consciousness can promote. Jung's point is that people inevitably hold themselves out in *some* way. Even the "See, I don't have a persona" way of holding oneself out is *also* a persona.

In Jung's analysis there are two dangers in the area of the persona. The first is having no adequately developed persona for a given situation, that is, being uncomfortable or inept or not socially adapted to a particular situation. A person without a persona feels naked, exposed, and vulnerable to the world. There is no adequate protection from the gibes or buffeting of others, and the outer expectations appear enormous and frightening. Such a person may withdraw from social contact in order to feel the needed protection.

The other danger Jung points out is the opposite—having a particular persona "glued" to the face. In this case identity is wrapped up wholly in the position in society. With a glued persona one is unable to separate oneself from the opinion others may have—for example, the leading soprano who is always *on stage* wherever she is or the clergyman who at home considers it a theologically inappropriate suggestion that he wash the dishes. Another example might be the stereotype of the doctor, who, at home or wherever, expects others to snap to attention and be subservient, just as the nurses and orderlies do at the hospital. The nurse who is always the nurse, doing his or her duty, but not feeling any need ever to take responsibility (since, at the hospital, responsibility is the doctor's job) has a glued persona. So does the counselor who always hears your casual comments as a problem to be solved or the professor who gives a lecture instead of conversation. Many professions carry a role identity, and over-identification with that role can cause glued-persona problems. Perhaps professions with "uniforms" are particularly fertile ground for such issues—notably the military and the clergy. A lot of clergy probably leave the ministry because of persona problems, not having worked out their own identity amidst the welter of expectations laid upon them. The clergy role provides an obvious identity, and when that need for identity is the reason for choosing the profession, you usually find a glued persona.

Parental expectations are customarily the source of the first persona patterns. In the beginning, the demands of the outside world and the parents appear to be the same; then a distinction must be learned. Ultimately, adequate psychological development entails the differentiation between ego and persona. There needs to be awareness of oneself as an individual apart from the external demands, and yet, at the same time, some adaptation needs to be made toward living compatibly with the outer world. Everyone needs a "flexible" persona—a different one for different occasions, just as there are different clothes for different occasions. It is not a matter of being hypocritical but of being responsive to a given situation without losing an inner sense of identity.

Interestingly, the dreams often present persona problems through the imagery of the clothes worn or not worn. The first year that we were studying Jung, an analyst from Zurich came to lecture at the Jung Center where we were studying. We had enjoyed chatting with him at a social following some of his talks, and we invited him to our home for tea one afternoon. This information is relevant because a visit to our home by a Jungian analyst was pretty heady stuff for us at the time, when the whole field of study still seemed so esoteric to us. It was this event which inspired Jean finally to write down a dream one morning—the first time she had done so. Jungians feel, quite rightly, that dreams remembered at such important times have special significance. This is the dream Jean wrote down the morning our guest was coming to tea:

> I was in a house. My mother was there. Some guests came and I was still in my pajamas, so I ran out and hid. I then went upstairs and went into a room to get something to put on.
>
> It was an extremely large room—huge—I couldn't see its sides and it was very, very still. There were some large plastic cases hanging on hangers. I knew that there were some dresses of mine stored there. In one plastic case where I looked there were a number of dresses of mine.
>
> One was a gold dress I had years ago, the one I had on when I was so embarrassed at that party. There were two which were my size, but they were exact replicas of dresses I made my daughters for their dolls last Christmas. I no longer remember the others.

This dream has several motifs of persona situations. First, the setting of a dream, as given in the first sentence or so, frequently gives an existing situation or context of the dream—in effect, the subject which the dream addresses. This dream suggests that Jean was at that time existing in a house with her mother—as we say in contemporary vernacular, "That's where she was coming from." This may mean one of two things, or even both. It may suggest that Jean was identified with some of the attitudes or practices of her own actual mother, or it may suggest that she was "caught in the mother"—either in her own role as a mother or in some unconscious patterns of behavior, as dark to her as the world is to a child still in the womb or too young to be consciously responsible. Either or all of these could be describing a persona situation—a persona identification with the archetype of conformity.

The next event in the story presents another common persona motif: Jean was inappropriately dressed for what happened. Sometimes in dreams the dreamer is completely naked when everyone else is dressed. Such dreams suggest that the dreamer is not adequately protected from the world, that the necessary security of an appropriate persona is lacking. So this imagery suggests that in some current situation Jean was experiencing (or perhaps fearing) she did not have an appropriate "way of being" in relation to others. Could the guests who came to her house be connected with the expected guest of the next day? It seems likely, and probably also the "guests" who were coming "into her house" were from the Jung studies—those visitors of the ideas new to her—and were troubling her with insecure feelings. How could these new ideas be reconciled with her adaptive persona as a clergy wife and leader of prayer and study groups? Jean didn't really know; she was still dressed for sleeping, not for waking up to new possibilities.

The drama does not stop there, however. She runs "upstairs" (up to the mind to try to think of new reconciling persona adaptations?) to look for something else to put on. This presents another common persona motif—looking for the right clothes, looking for something else to put on. When such a motif appears in a dream, it can be instructive to examine carefully what the associations are with the offered choices. In many cases, as in this dream, they seem to review possibilities which have been used in the past. Sometimes, probably in the forgotten dresses of this dream, there are new, future possibilities portrayed.

The gold dress which appeared from Jean's past was associated in her memory with a particularly painful evening from her university days, an evening when her behavior made her feel exposed as foolish— a memory connected with a shadow aspect (the archetype to be discussed in the next chapter). When she thought of the evening in relation to the persona, she realized that her behavior in the past arose out of her own sense of an inadequate persona—she didn't really know how to act—but instead of working with that problem sensibly, she had tried to cover up her insecurity with extraverted acting out and ended up feeling foolish. The appearance of this gold dress is a caution not to fall into the same error again. The other two dresses are replicas of doll dresses, which seems also to be a caution not to regress to a young, helpless, doll-like adaptation, but instead to move toward a genuine adult persona.

A similar motif appears in this dream of a forty-year-old woman:

> A group came to visit at the farm. Mom was there. She had ironed
> batches of toddler dresses. I could find no clothes to wear.

The dream suggests that the only relation to the outer world which her mother had prepared for her were toddler dresses—a too-young persona.

Wallace, during the time he was a parish priest, used to dream that he had arrived at the church without appropriate liturgical dress—a stole, for example. Though he liked the work of the parish priest, he would now understand such dreams as indicating that his truer calling lay elsewhere. In teaching he has made a more comfortable adaptation between the demands of the outer world and the movement of his own individuation.

It seems to us that much of the stress people experience in this stress-dominated culture comes from uncomfortable persona issues. This can arise from very small issues of discomfort as well as more far-reaching ones. When one moves into a new neighborhood or school or office, one is faced with making an entire new set of persona adaptations. Of course, previous experiences are helpful, but no matter how adjusted one has been, one still must use the persona with new people, which requires some energy. Until a comfort level is achieved in the new setting, one may find oneself cross and irritated about "nothing." Consciously facing such irritations as persona problems can give guidance and comfort until one is more at home.

Though persona problems may seem insignificant when compared to deeper aspects of individuation, they have more than surface significance. The person with either an inadequate persona adaptation or a rigid, glued-persona adaptation is blocked from moving on with the profound movements of life. Growth is stymied; transformation or change is terrifying.

The Nazi war criminal Eichmann is an example of how a role-identified nonpersonality failed to develop a personal, moral responsibility. He had no personal feelings or values of his own; he simply hid behind a collective morality in his obedience to his superiors. In the New Testament, Jesus is reported as repeatedly attacking the lack of individual responsibility. Often his confrontation with "the Pharisees" (the religious people of his day) is over a question of social conformity and *individual* responsibility.

The flexible persona permits one to be protected and yet open, responding to the movement of life in individually responsible ways.

•9

Shadow

Even more unknown than the persona to most people is their *shadow*. This is the term Jung used for the unconscious part of a person of which he or she is unaware and which has not been lived out. The wise have urged for centuries, "know thyself." Today many people are afraid that it is selfish and dangerously self-focused to spend time and energy in this endeavor, and, of course, attention *only* to oneself can be quite unproductive.

However, honest attention to the task of knowing oneself is beneficial. St. Theresa outlines the personal benefits for spiritual growth in the *Interior Castle*. She says that as we grow, we leave the old "rooms" behind and that the soul, in order to grow to the spaciousness of which it is capable, must be allowed to roam freely through all the "rooms" of its mansion, without being subjected to undue restraint or limitation. There is only one room that we should remain in all our lives, she tells us—the room of self-knowledge. She explains the reason for staying in this room with typically incisive humor—to help us stay humble. In other words, St. Theresa suggests that the continuing attention to knowing what is really in us leads us not to pride, but to its opposite, humility.

Jung and his followers have made the same discovery, and they further suggest that this kind of clear-eyed self-knowledge in more and more people is part of the process of making society as a whole more conscious and less liable to being swept away by mass hysteria.

In discussing the persona, we suggested that a flexible persona was a necessary development for everyone. One needs to relate to society in appropriate ways so as not to be too vulnerable. At the same time, one must never confuse the persona with genuine identity. Everyone needs to stay aware of those tendencies which are not so nice.

Children are taught very early not to show their more unpleasant or violent urges. They are even often admonished—alas—not to *feel* the emotions which in fact they do feel, as if they could simply turn off their feelings like the water in a faucet. Feelings themselves are facts and cannot thus be eliminated. Obviously, people need to be socialized; acting out their negative feelings can be harmful to them and to others. Yet what happens all too often is that they repress even the knowledge of their negative side until it is buried so deep they manage to forget its existence. They think their chosen conscious attitude is who they really are.

Yet this other side has not disappeared but only dropped into the unconscious, whence it can cause all sorts of trouble. The trouble frequently becomes painfully obvious when the shadow, as it were, forces its way into outer behavior. Then one may find, with great surprise, that one says exactly the opposite of what was "intended" or may "forget" the very papers needed to bring to the "important" meeting of "important" people. One protests vigorously that the intentions were otherwise, but Freud has taught that such "Freudian slips" have significance beyond conscious intention. Then the hidden embarrassing intentions, or, more often, the mixed motives, half of which were repressed, are forcibly brought to one's attention—and everyone else's attention as well.

The shadow appears in dreams as a figure of the same sex as the dreamer. As we said in discussing objective and subjective approaches to dreams, when people dream of someone they know, the dream may be about their outer, objective relationship to that person. However, when a same-sex figure is unknown to the dreamer or when the dream, interpreted on an objective level, is not helpful, the dream figure probably is a shadow figure. To identify the meaning of this shadow figure, one looks for the traits or attributes in the dream figure which are not in the conscious knowledge of the dreamer. This is personal amplification. Amplification from general sources—myths, fairy tales, literature—may also be helpful in understanding this unknown shadow aspect.

From whichever source, what one searches for is the significance for self-knowledge of the appearance of this particular shadow figure at this time. Once one becomes aware that the appearance of some person in dreams may be trying to call hidden traits to one's attention, it becomes unpleasant to wake some mornings and realize who the dream has been about—the initial reaction may well be "Oh, no!"

The shadow usually presents itself as an inferior or negative personality. These personifications of the inferior side which appear in dreams and myths are, Jung said, "the sum of all those unpleasant qualities we like to hide, together with the insufficiently developed functions and the contents of the personal unconscious."[1] The "realization of the shadow" is one of the steps Jung sees as being part of individuation, the process of becoming whole.

Frequently these unrecognized parts of the unconscious are observed as tendencies in other people, in the psychological process of "projection." Obviously, projections obscure the recognition of one's own unconscious traits—a built-in "protection" from seeing oneself clearly. Projections thus spoil the possibility of genuine human relationships and, if they are cultural, of whole groups of people—nationalities, races, political parties—who are then seen as "evil" or "dangerous." The result of projections is that part of one's personality remains on the "other side," but since there is some secret sympathy with this rejected part of the personality, one constantly and involuntarily does things which unwittingly help the "enemy."

Withdrawing projections is a difficult task and frequently requires some kind of psychic shock to create the courage and energy to do so. The drive of the shadowy part is so powerful as to be almost irresistible. Even after the determination to withdraw the projection is achieved, the task is by no means easy. Valiant repression is seldom the answer, nor is simply living out the impulses, which are frequently quite destructive. Important and valuable forces are frequently "contaminated" with the destructive forces, and in order to develop, the ego must assimilate these forces that are valuable, even though they may at first appear to be dark and evil by virtue of the destructive contamination. This is one of the most difficult ethical tasks of the individuation process.[2]

Jean experienced a rather serious manifestation of such an ethical task shortly after we returned from Zurich. The last trip we made during our stay in Europe was a pilgrimage to the Holy Land and Jerusalem, which in 1966 was split into two cities, one in Jordan and the other in Israel. In addition to the religious significance for us, Jean had felt a strong emotional affinity for the young Israeli nation as it made the desert bloom. Not long after our return to the U.S., the 1967 war broke out in the Middle East. There has been so much turmoil in the area since then, it may be hard to remember that particular war, but in that instance all the Arab nations around Israel had joined together with the avowed purpose of pushing Israel into the sea and destroying it. It seemed impossible that they would not succeed.

She sat glued to the television set with the United Nations debate broadcast continuously. As the tension grew, she felt a great sadness grow large in her, an almost mourning for that vigorous nation she had loved, together with an intense desire to be able to "do something about it." Suddenly, in the midst of that growing emotion which swept through her, she had a thought. It was such a shock to her that it drove everything else from her mind, yet despite her desire to do so, she could not deny to herself that the thought had been in her own mind, full blown and supported by intense feeling.

This was her thought: "I know what we could do. I have a final solution to this Arab problem!" Her full-blown thought meant, as it had for Adolph Hitler with reference to the Jews, that all the Arabs could be wiped out. What place had such a thought in the mind of a "good" Christian minister's wife who has just spent two years becoming more conscious in the Jung Institute?

The answer, of course, is that it had no place at all, but there it was—not to be denied or ignored. She knew in that moment that she "was" Hitler. The irony that her "final solution" was in defense of the very group Hitler had opposed was not lost on her. She had revealed to herself that she was not such a different person, potentially, from the great hater and destroyer of our century.

Such a psychic shock is not easy to accept. Yet the theory of depth psychology holds true even at such a moment—if such a shadow is there, it is better to know it than not to know it. If the possibility is recognized, then it can be worked with, whereas if such a content stays unconscious, then one may be possessed by it. "It has us instead of our having it," and the danger of being swept away by unacknowledged hatred and fear is all too real. Awareness and acknowledgement enable one to begin the ethical task of change.

In the smaller world of personal lives, many such shocks await the person who is not afraid to keep trying to know the shadow. The best clue to the existence of shadow aspects is the level of emotion about a given behavior. As we have suggested, the projections which happen to one are always accompanied by excessive emotion. You may have a fellow office worker, for example, whose bossiness is deplored by many people, but in a milder way than you react to it. If you find yourself churning with anger, unable to do your own work, inwardly rehearsing all the insulting things you would like to say to the bossy one, then you have a clue that there is just such a bossy one lurking within unbeknownst to you. Holding down the knowledge of that tendency or the behavior that goes with it may in fact be tying up much of your energy which could otherwise be used productively.

Many people get confused when they encounter the concept of projection; they will assert, "but that behavior *is* bad. Am I supposed to say it is all right?" Of course not. You can still make a value judgment that some behavior is destructive and wrong. The information that projection gives you is that you too are subject to the same temptations and tendencies. Then you are not quite so pleased with yourself. For example, if you discover that you too are susceptible to a secret race prejudice, you still deplore racist behavior, but you can no longer separate yourself from racists as though you were a different and better breed than they. You are then much closer to true humility, which the dictionary defines as having a modest sense of one's own significance.

The people on whom projections thrust themselves have some correspondence to the contents of those projections. They have a "hook" to catch the projections. The projections will continue to occur in a compulsive manner accompanied by intense emotion until the content becomes conscious. As one becomes more conscious of one's personal shadow qualities, one experiences the return of the energy which has been tied up in the repression. If the projection has exaggerated or distorted the projected shadow attribute in the person receiving the projection, one may then see the other person more accurately as well. Then a genuine personal relationship has a better chance to develop. The more one can perceive reality objectively, the less susceptible one is to infection from others, as, for instance, to mass psychology or mob reactions. One is better able to make truly moral judgments.

This aspect of the correspondence between seeing oneself more truly and thus relating more truly to others is poignantly expressed in this sonnet written by a former Denver resident, Steve Koneman, when he was fifteen years old:

I have become a silent spectator
locked inside an angry person
that hurls itself at any creator
to cause destruction without reason.
So from inside I wait for it to end
without control over this temper of his
And all the while I cannot comprehend
Who this other person really is.
If this person should turn out to be me
and his temper should be mine
Please forgive me for what I seem to be
It's me inside though I am hard to find.
And so I know this other is what I am.
Let me remember when I see it in another man.

Sometimes a shadow figure is elaborated over a period of time, and these figures can be of special help in coming to know oneself better. One woman first encountered an important shadow part of herself in a drawing she made of a rather prim Victorian lady with a pursed mouth. Since she knew that Jung regarded such drawings as significant (he said sometimes our hands will draw what our lips cannot say), she was puzzled by the sketch. Where did that lady come from? She regarded herself as a modern professional woman, though, like many, as one having occasional, rather irrational rages or depressions. For Sue, as we will call her, the process of getting acquainted with her Victorian lady was long and instructive.

Sue's initial personal association with "Victorian" was the stereotype of sexual repression for women and sexual license for men. She traced such patterns in her own family to her grandmother, who, she guessed, probably viewed sex something like the story of the premarital advice that Queen Victoria is supposed to have given her daughter about her wedding night: "Close your eyes and think of England!" Sex in her family, she felt, was probably viewed as a duty and burden for women. Yet she had considered herself far from this view: she had rejected it long before.

Even when one has consciously elected not to follow old family patterns, one may find pockets of unexamined opinions and behaviors lurking in the dark, and Sue began to discover some in herself. Some such pockets were rather trivial: in her family, the men always ordered the women's food in restaurants, for example. This can be experienced as a flattering attention, but Sue saw that she experienced it as a comment on female ineptitude and felt furious. Her rage was suggestive of hidden depths connected with the Victorian lady. Something about such habits made Sue feel, she said, like the Victorian corsets, which "sucked the women in" and bound them uncomfortably.

The next level which Sue uncovered in herself was a sense of uneasiness when any man appeared to be attracted to her. Even if the encounter had no apparent sexual overtones, Sue experienced great discomfort. Somehow, she felt as if she were not all right.

She then began to see that she felt as if it were not all right if she got promoted or if she sought professional advancement to a more responsible position. Starting with the Victorian primness, she acted as if women were inferior to men. Though she did not accept this idea intellectually, she continually sabotaged herself professionally; there was within Sue a secret Victorian lady who managed to "keep her in her place." As she followed these patterns and feelings to increasing depths in herself and looked at the other women in her family, Sue discovered that they were symbolic of a pattern of serious failures of the women to live genuine lives. She saw that her mother and her mother's sisters had all failed, really, to *live*.

The fear which Sue had first experienced as vaguely sexual was shown to be far more inclusive. Something in the entire feminine pattern had said to Sue, deep within herself, that it was not all right to be oneself and to be honest. What had looked like a simple sexual denial was much more complex—a block to Sue's living her life fully from all those unlived women's lives of the past. Needless to say, such a block not only interfered with her genuine relationships but held her bound to being only a small part of who she could be and felt called to be. She became afraid of "going on," whatever that entailed for her. Sue's reflections on the Victorian lady had led her far beyond any simplistic and trivial connections with only her sexuality (though that was involved), but, even more, to the completion within herself of the search for her own fully lived life.

This is quite a good example of how limiting it can be to interpret a symbol only as a sign. If Sue's initial associations with Victorian views on sexuality had been taken as pointing only to sexuality, she might have stopped her work with the Victorian lady at her own sex life instead of continuing to plumb the depths of the myriad effects such limiting views can have on all of life. Then she might have thought that all her problems would be solved if only she could learn some new sexual techniques or find satisfying sexual partners—a primrose path of frustration.

At various stages along the explorations, Sue had dreams with helpful motifs of transforming possibilities. Some of these involved positive animus figures engaged in the search with Sue (for which topic, see chapter 11). In one such dream, her positive animus figure lay ill in a Victorian house. The "house" where one lives frequently suggests the set of attitudes one holds at the time. In subsequent scenes of the same dream, Sue "worked on wholeness," "felt successful," and went on a long journey at night over the sea, among ice floes, which were dangerous and treacherous, but she was safe. This is a cautious, but very optimistic set of images for the journey to her own wholeness which Sue had set out on. The feeling of "success" was probably an early clue, had it been spotted, of the nuances of meaning of "Victorian" for her.

In a humorous symbol, when Sue was feeling quite discouraged and low on energy, she dreamed that another positive animus figure, her husband this time, had put a "transformer" in a tiny room in an old Victorian building. He told her that even if the room was so hot it was not usable when the transformer was turned on, it was necessary and could not be moved. She needed to stay with her transformation process, despite the "heat."

In other Victorian houses in other dreams, Sue was "reassured about her credentials," borrowed some clothes, did an exotic dance in costume, studied with three others to pass an examination. In yet another dream, an unknown woman wearing Victorian pantaloons announced, "I'm going to change." All of these dreams and others began to show Sue the depth with which the lack of honesty about herself (which shows up when she fears letting herself know she has done something well) is a false and destructive pattern. These insights all began with an unknown and unsuspected shadow figure which emerged from a pencil sketch.

Thus far we have focused on the negative aspects of the shadow. Part of Jung's insight into the unconscious contents, however, as we have noted, was the observation that positive, creative potential of the individual may also arise from the unconscious. It also frequently occurs that unrecognized *positive* traits may show up in dream figures or in projections. Surprisingly, the integration of these traits may be as difficult as the negative ones.

The clues are similar: the appearance of a same-sex figure in a dream or the intensity of the emotional reaction to someone in a projection, only in this case the emotions are of admiration. It seems to be as hard to own the possibility of the "good" that is seen in others as it is to own the "bad." Clergy and professed religious feel the weight of these positive projections frequently. It is as if people who are unwilling or fearful of carrying their own spiritual development try to make the professional carry it for them. They are not owning their own positive qualities, but laying them on others. This seems to us to account for the level of fury which parishioners feel when they find their clergy being less than their idealizations. Another interesting development currently is the withdrawal of the projections society had made onto the medical profession of the responsibility to make everyone well. The wellness movement stresses the individual responsibility for health in a way that could not have been foreseen a few short years ago.

The realization of the shadow is pictured in a charming form in the dream of a woman who had been at work on seeing her shadow and "cleaning it up" during a couple of years of dream work when she had this dream:

> Someone angrily threw a wet rag in my face, after she finished some cleaning. I went to the washroom to wash my hands, and she followed, throwing the rag at me again. "You know, don't you," I said, "that the reason it bugs us so is that we each see ourselves in the other? So let's kiss ourselves," and I kissed her.

The image of the cleaning rag being thrown again and again at the dreamer's face is a vivid reminder of how unpleasant it feels to engage in this endless dialogue with the shadow, no matter how positive the values uncovered.

A potent artistic expression of the integration of the shadow despite its unacceptable surface is Galway Kinnell's poem "Saint Francis and the Sow":

> The bud
> stands for all things,
> even for those things that don't flower,
> for everything flowers, from within, of self-blessing;
> though sometimes it is necessary

to reteach a thing its loveliness,
to put a hand on its brow
of the flower
and retell it in words and in touch
it is lovely
until it flowers again from within, of self-blessing;
as Saint Francis
put his hand on the creased forehead
of the sow, and told her in words and in touch
blessings of earth on the sow, and the sow
began remembering all down her thick length,
from the earthen snout all the way
through the fodder and slops to the spiritual curl
    of the tail,
from the hard spininess spiked out from the spine
down through the great broken heart
to the blue milken dreaminess spurting and shud-
    dering
from the fourteen teats into the fourteen mouths
    sucking and blowing beneath them:
the long, perfect loveliness of sow.[3]

Animals are closer to their instincts than most people, and in dreams they represent a more instinctual, less conscious part of the shadow.

The same image occurred in this dream of a reserved, quiet, controlled, woman who worked as a secretary:

I was in a bedroom which at first seemed like the bedroom I shared with my sister when we were children. In a pen in the corner of the room, there was a rather wild-looking pig that was rooting at the corner of the pen, breaking the boards. The pig's snout was covered and sort of dripping with foaming saliva—sort of like a mad dog. The pig succeeded in breaking through the bars of the pen. As we tried to get it into a bathroom, we couldn't keep it there because the doors did not have locks or latches, and the animal ran out.

Then we tried to get it into a long narrow room that was like a sun porch. At this point, I think my sister wanted to call my father from next door for help. But we decided "no" because he was sick and frail, and I think one of us tried to dial an emergency number on the telephone.

However, at this point, the pig dashed out the front door, running down the street, and it seemed to turn into a woman with long flying hair and white filmy dress or scarf streaming out behind her as she ran down the street.

The dreamer associated the dream with pig traits which she deplored, and she greatly feared that the dream meant there was a dirty, rabid, slop-eating pig inside of her. In fact, she was a rather fastidious, stylish, dainty person—so the dream probably has some compensatory function for her outer persona.

On closer examination, however, she saw that the pig was only a pig as long as it was penned up. When it got out of the house where it could run freely, it became the running woman in white. This pig was evidently a very old pattern in her, because the dream took place in her childhood bedroom. This gave a good starting place to look for the parts of herself that she secretly deplored as piglike, as well as holding out the hope for transformation of those qualities when they were let out—that they could be humanized and become beautiful— an image from her unconscious like the "long, perfect loveliness" of the poem.

As one tries to learn the value hidden in the shadow, the pearl can be a helpful image. The pearl itself is created when something like a bit of grit gets inside the oyster, and the oyster begins to build up layers of protection against the pain the grit causes. Slowly, layer by layer, in secrecy and silence, the pearl is formed. Sometimes it may seem that the darkness could never be beautiful, but the black pearl is the most valuable of all. The transformation of the shadow can be a pearl for any life if one learns, with the sow, the long, perfect loveliness of that which was formerly despised.

• 10

Anima

The "other side" of the psyche (the unconscious) is represented in dreams not only by same-sex figures (the shadow), but also by figures of the opposite sex. From analyzing thousands of dreams, Jung observed that these figures of the opposite sex played a distinctive role in the psyche. Just as both men and women have both male and female genes biologically, Jung thought that psychologically there was a corresponding contrasexual reality. This reality, he theorized, is represented by these opposite-sex dream figures.

Jung used the term *anima* for the feminine figure in a man's unconscious and the term *animus* for the male figure in women's dreams. Both terms are the Latin word for soul or spirit, with different gender endings. The term itself suggests something of the distinctive role which Jung felt these figures played in one's personality.

There are two ways of being human—male and female—and every individual has aspects or qualities of both. During the long course of human history some aspects of what it means to be human have been exercised more by one sex than the other and so have become associated more with that sex than the other. In the contemporary world there is less differentiation of roles and tasks. Just what influence this fact will have on the appearance of the contrasexual figures in dreams remains to be seen. Some duality is obviously present in all of life, aside from sex: active-passive, light-dark, wet-dry, good-evil, cold-hot. An interpenetration of the opposites is a part of life. Anima-animus differentiation is one way of approaching this duality in human experience. It is not, however, just a theoretical concept for Jung. He found the duality in dreams. Furthermore, the personification experienced in the dreams is helpful in identifying and bringing to consciousness those aspects and qualities of the individual personality so represented.

As noted earlier, same-sex or shadow figures in dreams are representations of qualities or tendencies that are unconscious. Contrasexual dream figures are another way the unconscious is manifested in dreams. The anima for a man is, in a sense, a "deeper layer" in the unconscious than the shadow. She is more difficult to recognize, more of a "mystery" to him, as indeed, the opposite sex usually is. A man knows what it is like to be a man; he cannot in the same way know what it is like to be a woman. "Woman," Jung said, "with her very dissimilar psychology, is and always has been a source of information about things for which a man has no eyes."[1] Hence, the anima seems to serve the distinctive function of leading a man to the depths of his soul.

In its individual manifestation, Jung said, the character of a man's anima is usually shaped by his mother. If that relationship was a positive one, the woman who becomes his wife may be startled to recognize, usually in later life, that she has many of the qualities of her mother-in-law. A man, in his love-choice, frequently is strongly tempted to win the woman who best corresponds to his own unconscious femininity and who can thus receive his projection of his own soul. Mature development of such a relationship requires the withdrawal of his projections and seeing a woman as she really is. Our own experience illustrates the point. We had not been in Zurich and under way with our analysis long before we could see that our own marriage had been a rather clear case of a mutual anima-animus projection, for we got engaged on our third date, one week after our first date, having met only casually three months earlier. There was no way we could really have known each other. One of our friends, practicing in the same large law firm with us, remarked at the time: "I know both of them better than they know each other, but I think they will like each other after they get to know each other." He was right, in a wonderful way, but it did require work.

The image of the anima is formed not only from a man's personal encounters with woman during his early years, but also, Jung felt, there was "an imprint or 'archetype' of all the ancestral experiences of the female, a deposit, as it were, of all the impressions ever made by woman."[2]

The experience of the anima takes both negative and positive forms. In the Jungian literature one often finds the negative anima given more attention. The negative anima is perhaps more easily recognized and can create the problems that cause one to seek help. Negative aspects of the anima are indicated when a man is moody, touchy, sensitive, easily irritated and his personal relationships with others are in disarray. It was Jung's observation that there seemed to be occasions when a man, in an "anima mood," behaved like the culture's stereotypical idea of an unpleasant woman—an "inferior" woman.

The following dream illustrates the appearance of a negative anima figure and perhaps a positive one whom he does not yet know. The dreamer is a young man who reported that he went to bed on Halloween night, having decided not to go to several parties to which he had been invited. He did not want to be bothered, and generally, he said, he was in a "bad mood." He recorded this dream:

> I'm walking by what seems to be an apartment building. There is a young unknown girl standing outside the back door. I ask her if Mrs. B lives there. "Yes," she says, "I'll get her." "Never mind," I say. I walk by, but turn around as I hear my name being called. It is Mrs. B. I shake hands with her and notice that she's dressed in a black skirt and blouse. She asks me what I'm doing. I reply that I'm planning on returning to school full time in the fall. She begins saying how the world situation looks bleak, there's too much to be pessimistic about—she goes on in this manner for some time.

The multiple dwelling in which Mrs. B lives would suggest that she is associated with some collective opinions rather than individual ones. The dreamer meets a young girl outside the "back door." He asks her a question, but then rejects her response and moves on. His refusal of the help offered by a young girl his age may connect to his own mood, with no clear idea of what was wrong or how to explore his sense of discontent. When addressed by Mrs. B, he shakes hands with her and enters into a conversation. Her black clothes, bleak outlook, and generally pessimistic views seem to reflect the dreamer's attitude at the time.

We also have a clue to his mood in the conflict between his stated intention (in the dream) to return to school and Mrs. B's discouragement of his decision. The dream thus suggests that he is torn between his ego decision and some unconscious fears about the future. If the unknown girl is a positive anima figure, her function for his future is not yet clear. However, Jung's theory suggests that such figures lead men to their own individual meaning.

The following dream of a graduate student in psychology suggests the situation of a young man who was just beginning to get in touch with his inner feminine side, perhaps through his part-time work in a clinic to help young people. He cared deeply about his work, even as the dream suggests:

> I was at an underprivileged high school to talk to the students and get their reactions on having the Open Clinic come to discuss drug use and abuse. I was speaking to many minority kids while they were going from classroom to classroom. Some of them were opposed to having the Clinic speak, but most were enthusiastic. I approached two girls and began explaining who I was and what the Open Clinic was planning on doing. They were very excited about the idea. I soon found out that one of the girls was a runaway with no place to live. She wanted me to take her to the Clinic to find her a place to stay. We went outside to get my car, but when we got there it had been stolen. I rushed into the nearest store and phoned the police.

The dream indicates his interest in responding to the young girl who needs a "place to stay." However, he finds his car has been stolen, and he has, for the time being, no way to take her with him. In reporting the theft, the dream seems to say he is trying to handle the situation. The dreamer said that the loss of his car in the dream suggested to him his "lack of personal energy or experience, even though I was attempting to assist."

Coming to terms with his anima can lead a man to a deeper level of integration, providing him with inspiration as well as giving him a more balanced view of life. She, like other archetypal figures, can also carry the energy to complete the needed tasks, as the young man's association with the dream above suggests. This function can perhaps be seen in a story about the composer Berlioz. It is said that at about the age of twenty-one he saw a red-haired Irish Shakespearean actress and was completely entranced by her. While in the throes of the enchantment, he wrote *Symphonie Fantastique*, based on his fantasy of their meeting in a romanticized fashion, his eventually killing her, and his being marched to the gallows for her death. Actually, he later met and married her, but the marriage was not a success and did not last. The inner figure is for our inner journey; and when we try to find it exclusively outside, it doesn't always work, for when the projection is withdrawn, there may be nothing left.

The anima can be for a man the "one who shows the way" to his own inner spiritual development. In literature, the classic example of the positive anima is Dante's Beatrice. Dante really never knew Beatrice; he first saw her when she was eight and he was nine. Yet she was for him the source of his vision and inspiration. He was able to turn this outer experience of an ideal woman into his work. His love *became* his work, and he did his work for love.

When a man wants to understand the practical meaning of the anima as guide to his inner world, he must begin by taking seriously the feelings, moods, expectations, and fantasies sent by his anima. As he works patiently and slowly at giving this attention, other more deeply unconscious material wells up from the depths and connects with the earlier material. This is a crucial part of his individuation process, but it is a slow, lifetime process and requires conscious work.

In the history of Western culture one could say that the medieval knightly cult of the lady signified a first attempt to differentiate the feminine side of man's nature in regard to the outer woman as well as in relation to the inner world. This medieval worship of women presided, Jung said, over the birth of modern individualism, since it meant the worship of his soul.[3] As a personification of his anima, the lady could teach the knight to differentiate both his own feelings and his behavior toward women.

Avoidance of anima development can occur when one ignores the aspect of the anima as one who can teach significantly and, instead, views her as an exclusively personal being. Then she is projected on to someone in the outer world and her meaning can only be found there. A man then becomes "either the victim of his erotic fantasies or compulsively dependent on one actual woman."[4] The anima has no inner meaning for him, and his inner process of individuation stagnates. Then he thinks his problems can only be solved in the outer world— not by any change within. At this point, a man may decide that if he could only leave his wife and be with another woman all would be well.

The basic problem the anima presents, Jung said, is always one of relationships. She frequently carries the feelings which a man represses as "un-masculine," but which are a needed part of him. His feelings become infantile and sentimental when they are repressed, yet such feelings are related to his personal values. Coming into a relationship with his anima also means a man is less sensitive about revealing any weakness to others.

Here is the first dream brought to his counselor by a divorced businessman in his early forties:

> I was on a dish-shaped capsule which was part of a gondola ride at an amusement park. I was alone, but in the capsule next to me was a woman. We engaged in pleasant talk. She was an artist and was painting inside the capsule. One painting was of a face which was familiar, but I couldn't put a name on it. We were motionless. The ride had stopped.
>
> We were in my kitchen. The same woman was sitting on the kitchen counter, in a corner. I began kissing her softly. She was pleased.

The "initial dream" when one decides to do some inner work is frequently indicative not only of the current situation but also of the possible future course of development. Such was the case here.

The dreamer had come for counseling because of a dawning awareness that he was separated from his feminine side. He tended to experience ambivalent projections of his anima in the outer world and he wanted to work on this issue. The woman in the dream was unknown to the dreamer and has the qualities, the dream suggests, of a creative artist. She is painting a face which was familiar, but which he could not name. Perhaps his anima is even painting the "face" he can be. In the opening situation "the ride had stopped"; they were motionless. Then the scene changes, perhaps suggesting the next step which has begun or is about to begin. They are in the dreamer's kitchen—a place of transformation, where the raw is changed into the cooked—and he kisses the unknown woman softly. She is pleased. This suggests a good prognosis for his inner journey. He is ready to begin relating in a transformative way to his own feminine inner woman.

The appearance of the anima in dreams or fantasies is an autonomous activity of the unconscious, representing a coming to life of something unconscious, an animated psychic atmosphere.[5] The anima then represents a spontaneous movement toward life—to the life of concreteness, of earth, of emotionality, directed toward people and things. The anima then can lead a man toward involvement and an instinctual connectedness to other people and to a containing community or group.

This positive role of the anima is suggested in the dream of a man we will call Terry. Terry was a professional man, in mid-life, talking of marriage with Amy. He was torn with indecision, terrified of being "scolded," and feeling that he couldn't shoulder more responsibility—both economic and emotional. Yet he was also sometimes swept with the thought that his life would have no meaning if Amy left him. In point of fact, he tended to overdramatize his inability to work and his lack of competence. Then he had the following compensatory dream:

> Amy and I are in some strange mountain city. We are leaders of some kind, punishing all the bad fascist kind of people. We are like a two-man vigilante team. I don't know what it is we did, but it required incredible endurance, leadership, daring and resourcefulness on both our sides. It required confrontation and daring and courage—many people admired us, and many threatened and hated us, but we were brave and courageous and faced the consequences unafraid.

The dream says that when he was with Amy he was a leader, with daring and courage. Terry's task became one of recognizing that regardless of how special Amy was in outer life, when he was in relationship with his "Amy-within," he was a leader who could face any consequences unafraid.

Jung said that when a man was young, he could afford to lose his anima for a time, as his important task was to free himself from the mother and become a man. In later life the continued loss is destructive:

> After the middle of life, however, permanent loss of the anima means a diminution of vitality, of flexibility, and of human kindness. The result, as a rule, is premature rigidity, crustiness, stereotypy, fanatical one-sidedness, obstinacy, pedantry, or else resignation, weariness, sloppiness, irresponsibility, and finally a childish *ramollissement* with a tendency to alcohol.[6]

The desire for new and different undertakings can make itself felt first in the form of a vague impulse or mood or an unclear emotional yearning. This unconscious stirring in a man may be embodied in a feminine image. The dreamer in the following dream is a man who, at mid-life, decided he needed to work on an inner journey through some spiritual counseling. He had a longing for more meaning in his life, though he had a busy life as a successful businessman. He recounted this dream:

The dreamer is in a restaurant, standing in line. He begins to wipe great gobs of butter on the skirt of a girl standing in the line. It bothered her, but she said nothing. He talked to her and got along with her O.K.

Then he left the store with a colleague from work—the Controller of his office—and someone else (a male) from the office, to go to an airplane. The dreamer's pants were off, and he had to run back into the restaurant. He saw a married couple he had known and admired as a boy—a real lady and gentleman, who were calm, cool and collected. He wanted to talk to them, but he was too late and had to hurry. He said goodbye to the butter girl, feeling sexual attraction and a warm relationship with her. He touched her hand.

This dream is a good example of how dreams sometimes make puns or word-plays. This dreamer had thought that he was going to take steps to work on his inner life, but he hadn't really made a commitment. The dream says: you're just "buttering up" the anima, and she suffers in silence. Then the dream reminds him of his admiration of a couple (a picture of what his own wholeness could be like), but he keeps rushing off with the "Controller" from his office. The business side of his life is in control. He was standing in line for food, but he couldn't wait for it. Food in a dream frequently represents spiritual nourishment. There was also a persona problem—he didn't have his pants on as he left the restaurant. Perhaps his sense that his relation to the outer world was not clear made him feel undressed, driving him back inside to the positive images. He was drawn to his anima, and at least he touched her hand. Yet the feeling of the dream is that he is not ready to stay with her.

The appearance of the anima, who, as indicated, is connected with finding the way toward meaning, occurs frequently when all meaning is threatened or lost. The situation is characterized, Jung said, "by the more or less sudden collapse of a form or style of life which till then seemed the indispensable foundation of the individual's whole career."[7] The anima may be discerned in a dream figure, as indicated above, or may be recognized in a projection on a woman in the outer world. In the latter case, the task involves, as discussed earlier, seeing through one's projections and recognizing the nature of the anima.

Generally speaking, Jung said, the intensity of a projection is equivalent to the importance of the projected content, which is always an activated unconscious that seeks expression.[8] The method of withdrawing a projection is to detach it completely from the image to which it has been attached and recognize that it belongs to oneself. This involves acknowledging the "symbolic value" of the object, which effectively restores the meaning imbedded in the symbol back to oneself.[9] Withdrawing a projection on a woman in the outer world or recognizing the role of an inner feminine dream figure enables a man to enter a new relationship with his unconscious. In Jung's terms, he has a new relationship with his anima.

•11

Animus

The *animus*, as we have indicated, is Jung's term for the masculine aspect of woman. The relation of masculine and feminine in women and men is the area of Jungian theory which is being challenged and questioned more than any other today. It is a rare issue of a Jungian journal that does not have at least one article addressing the question. While most of the writers honor Jung for his early insight into the significance of contrasexual figures, few still accept his total "package" of listed characteristics of what "masculine" and "feminine" mean.

These new explorations, like much of the consciousness-raising involved in the women's movement, are changing general attitudes, however slowly. Despite all this, there is little clarity as yet about what the basic differences in gender signify psychologically. Perhaps it is appropriate to paraphrase scripture and say, "It doth not yet appear what we shall be."

In whatever ways understanding is enlarged or changed, in the meantime, women keep dreaming about these figures, and Jungian thought does have some helpful clues about how they can be understood. Traditional associations with the masculine principle are with action, focus, and power; and those can give a good starting place. As with all dream figures, the general meaning can serve as a backdrop while attention is primarily directed toward the particular image in each dream. An animus figure in a dream raises such questions as these: to what particular consciousness is this animus figure pointing? What special action is he leading the dreamer toward? What new creativity or potential within this particular dreamer is he calling attention to? Or, with a negative animus figure, one can ask: what rigidity, obstinacy,

79

absolute convictions, or sense of personal nullity does he embody so that the dreamer can see the danger toward which she is headed? Like all archetypes, the animus carries the energy to enable the person to follow through, but coming to see these truths is very difficult and requires hard work.

The detailed examination of a series of dreams which Jean had when we first began to study Jung illustrates several aspects of the kind of development and transformation the animus carries. The first dream occurred shortly after Jean began her Jungian study. At this time, Wallace was a parish priest, and Jean was engaged in home, family, and the leadership of several prayer and study groups in the church. She felt a wary interest in Jung, but was fearful of its compatibility with Christianity.

> I was in a mansion and a very tall, very blond, broad-shouldered man and I were going in to a buffet. We looked in on a gigantic banquet hall where there were tables up on long platforms set with gleaming services—enough for hundreds to eat.
>
> My blond suggested we go eat. They were the most sumptuous tables I've ever seen. I selected more and more and more—just getting all I really wanted! (In waking life, I was dieting at the time.) There were waiters who carried your plates to the tables, so we had our hands free, and we held hands as we walked along.
>
> As we walked "outside," where we had decided to eat, I was thinking—if he asks me to marry him, I will. I was conscious of a surging sexual attraction to him and of a real physical reaction. Then he said, "Will you get a divorce and marry me?" I had forgotten I was married! Thrown into great distress, I began to mutter, "Oh, I couldn't!" I wanted badly to kiss his hand. I thought: someone will see me, but I don't care. I kissed his hand very lovingly just as we came into the sun. As I raised my head, I looked into the eyes of one of our parishioners. She raised her eyebrows.
>
> I was thinking frantically—I've got to have him. I began to plan whether I could have an affair with him. I'd think how I just had to. Then I'd think of Wallace and of confession and of honesty and of what it would do to all of it—but I was such a consuming fire of desire that I knew it was a real possibility.

At the time of this dream, Jean had no notion what it meant. The blond man was completely unknown to her, and, nurtured on Freud's theory of wish-fulfillment without even knowing where it came from, she was afraid someone would tell her she was longing to have an affair, though it certainly did not seem so to her. Her only contact with someone who interpreted dreams was in a group class, and she was by no means ready to present this dream to a group. So it stayed there in her dream book as a puzzle to her.

With the advantage of hindsight, it seems to refer to all the "sumptuous feast" that Jung's thought has been for her in the years since that time. Some deep part of her had a "consuming fire of desire" for that richness. The parishioner who raises her eyebrows is a shadow image of the part of Jean which was holding back from this "illicit" attraction. Probably even Wallace in the dream represents her marriage to Christianity and her view that the study might somehow threaten her honest devotion to that (though Wallace himself at the time was pressing forward with the study, unbothered by the sort of worry Jean had). The fear of being untrue to Wallace-as-animus and her real love seems to be the image of the dream.

Shortly after that dream, we received a joint grant for study at the Jung Institute in Zurich and moved there with our three children. After three months of study and analysis, Jean had this dream:

> I went to Gewerbeschule class one night without Wallace for some reason. During the lesson my teacher kept looking at me very often. I was in a wild fever of physical longing for him, and I wondered if he had any of this same feeling. However, I also tried to look somewhat proper, though it was hard. Then we were to do our written exercises, and I went a little away from the others in the class. He came out where I was and began to talk to me. The more he talked, the more excited I became; and my body was a great storm of longing.
>
> Then finally he looked at me and said, "Every woman I meet must learn from me or she must sleep with me. Which shall you do?" I wanted to sleep with him so badly that I could hardly bear it—most difficult. I paused a long while and then I could hardly make my mouth say the words. Finally, with pauses between the words, I was able to wring out in gasps, "I must learn from you." I could not look at him while I said it. He was staring hard at me and finally he said something curt to the effect that he accepted my reply, but in some way he managed to convey that he wondered if I did. He whirled and left.

As you will perceive, the situation was now somewhat different. For Jean the pressure was high. This dream concerned a man she actually knew and saw twice weekly, and (from her viewpoint), even worse, she was now in analysis, and taking her dreams in for interpretation. She entertained wild thoughts of suppressing this dream, which embarrassed her, but finally decided that if she was going to be in this "mess" called analysis, she might at least do it honestly. So, under some inner stress, she read the dream to her analyst.

He began, quite properly, with the objective possibilities. Are you in Gewerbeschule class? —Yes, we are taking lessons in German language. Is the man in this dream in fact your teacher? —Yes, he is. Are you in love with your German teacher? —Oh, no! I think he is nice, but he is not even particularly attractive to me.

He probed around a bit more, probably to decide whether or not Jean was really just trying to hide her attraction for this man from him or even from herself. Evidently satisfying himself that this was not the case, he then said, "Well, then, he must be an inner animus figure for you. Tell me what he is like." Because Jean could not reach into herself enough at that time to know, they got little further than that. The analyst did open her to the insight, though, that something which that German teacher represented to her was a deep longing of her heart— to learn about, yes, but even further, to merge with and make an important part of her life. It was actually fifteen years later that Jean finally saw one important aspect of the dream. The German teacher was also a teacher of literature, working on his doctorate. By the time Jean made this connection, she had just completed her doctorate in literature, and that literary study has been a door for her not only to the enjoyment of literature for itself, but also as a deepening of her understanding of symbolic process.

The third and last dream in the series came after a year of study at the Jung Institute. It has a more distanced quality, with unreal aspects as compared to the ordinary reality of the first two, perhaps suggesting a deeper, more mythic importance for her life.

> There was a woman who was going with a man. Then another man came up and met her and loved her at once. She loved him too, but she felt they had to hide from the other man because she was afraid of him. There were several incidents where he tried to catch the new man, but they always managed to hide him or let him escape without detection.
>
> Finally one day she was in a large drugstore with room for dancing, when the new man came. She wanted him to leave, as the old man was due to come, but he said he was tired of running

away. They began to dance together so closely that their bodies merged as though they had no clothing. They knew they belonged together and were nearly one now.

Then the other man arrived and in a tense scene, began to chase the new man. The new one gracefully avoided and taunted his charges laughingly. The whole chase assumed a similarity to a bull fight. Finally the new man was injured, and the other ran away. She ran to him and began to care for him, openly declaring herself now that he was threatened with danger. She tried to get a male friend in the crowd to go for help, but he said, "No, the authorities will come and I want to be here to tell them what happened. I saw it all, and we will get the other man out of the way once and for all." So they sat, waiting for the authorities to come.

This powerful dream, as it was for her, is a clear confrontation between her "old" set of attitudes, of which she was afraid, and her "new" set of possibilities with which she was "nearly one now." The dream suggests that she is hiding something from a part of herself, or, put another way, being controlled by some part of herself which keeps her from being open about her love.

A drugstore, where the confrontation takes place, is a place where one gets healing medicine, and this one is most unusual—one with room for dancing! This dance of life is a strong indication that the new way is positive for her, as she knows deep within her that they belong together. The merger in the dream was part of the unreal quality, as it was an actual bodily merger, rather than intercourse, but her feelings of ecstasy were strong. The courage and laughing gaiety of the new man are other factors which set him up clearly as a positive figure. Then, when he is injured, she finally declares herself openly. The injury probably refers to the fact that the conflict in Jean, most of which she kept under wraps, had grown so strong that she had suddenly terminated her analysis, for the reason that she was just "too tired." This tiredness was real, as the conflicts within us as we fight off some potentials for transformation can be enervating in the extreme.

One interesting aspect of the dream concerns the language with which it ends. Jean thought about police, but she wrote "authorities," as the dream said. Dream language can thus show us where our reality lies, because she was in truth waiting for some sense of her inner authority to sort out the bits and pieces of her meaning which needed sorting.

A similar pattern of fear of change coupled with excitement about new visions and possibilities occurs in two dreams of a Roman Catholic religious sister. At the end of a year's special study course in renewal, she saw the two aspects of herself, her new directions and her conservative animus, resisting the change in this dream:

> I go to visit a sick and very conservative bishop. I even take Holy Communion to him, but he says, "No." I take the Blessed Sacrament home.

This sister was authorized by the church to administer the sacrament, but it would have been unusual for a woman—who cannot be ordained under the present regulations of that church—to take the sacrament to a bishop! This sister, however, after her own spiritual growth during her year of special study, was being invited to help other people—men and women—in ways which her own conservative leanings still considered to be the sole prerogative of an ordained priest. The dream seems to picture this conflict between the two parts of herself—her conscious ego and a "sick and very conservative" authoritative animus figure within her.

A year later she had a dream which seemed to her to point to a coming together of the conservative and the person open to new things, in the image of another conservative authority figure, a monsignor whom she knew in waking life, giving his blessing to the "progressive."

> I dreamed I was preparing for ordination. We were a mixed group of men and women, and it was up to us to decide if we would go ahead. At the last minute I was confused. We were in the church waiting to begin the service for ordination, and I went over and asked to see the Monsignor. I needed to confirm my decision with someone, and he was the teacher of the class. We talked, and I told him of my doubts. He didn't say much. Finally I said, "Do you feel I'm right in going ahead?" He said, "Yes." I was relieved, and we returned to the ceremony, being late. We got there just at the end of the queue for imposition of hands. Monsignor laid hands on my head.

From this dream experience, the sister felt the actual sense of relief the dream refers to; some of her inner conflict was peacefully settled.

Sometimes an initial dream is of special importance, as we have said. One very short dream came to a woman the night before her first hour to do dream work with Jean. She had previously met both of us at a weekend workshop.

> I was at Jean Clift's house at a very good pot-luck. Wallace was serving all the good food. Very pleasant.

Her associations with Wallace, as the dream indicates, were very pleasant. The fact that he was the one preparing and serving the food indicates that the dream work will probably focus on animus questions, and the area toward which her attention will fruitfully turn at this point in her life is toward an exploration of her power and meaning, reexamining any opinionated rigidities she may hold toward herself or others. Further work will show the specific direction of those explorations.

Sometimes dreams are quite explicit in pointing toward animus concerns. An amusing and important dream of this type came to a woman in her early forties who had been reared to be a typical belle in the deep south. At the time of the dream, her marriage had failed, and she was the single parent of two teen-age children. She was also a successful professional woman, but her self-doubt continually attacked her, and she herself could not see her professional or personal value. It seemed always to her that she needed someone else to proclaim her value to her, especially a man who would love her. Yet she liked her work, except for the attacks of depression, and possessed a bright and inquiring mind interested in many things. After working with her dreams and with these issues for a couple of years, she had the following transformative dream:

> I am with two friends, a couple (the man is quick-tempered and hateful, says hateful things to people; the woman discounts herself, is a typical southern belle). The man is driving, and his wife is in front. I'm in the backseat.
>
> We are leaving the ranch or farm, but have to go through a structure like a barn. At this moment a man appears in the doorway with a sawed-off shotgun. He does threatening, menacing kinds of things for a while, then makes it plain that he wants me and intends to do me harm (rape maybe). I'm feeling terrified when I suddenly realize that he is acting out, word for word, a play that I have written and that the gun isn't loaded. I say, "The gun isn't loaded." We all laugh kind of nervously. He just shrugs his shoulders, lowers the gun and walks around muttering to himself. There is a feeling of great relief among all three of us.

Relief there was indeed for the dreamer, who knew that the dream had come from within her and must have some truth for her. The feeling tone of the dream and its striking language opened her to seeing the reality that she was in fact creating the danger for herself; she herself had written the lines he said in the play. The gun was not loaded and could do her no real harm, except as she gave him power by her fear.

It was also instructive to see the parallels in the couple who were literally "driving her around"—in charge of where she went in life and how she got there. Taken as parts of herself, the man was like her own negative inner animus voice which continually was hateful; the woman was like her own shadow behavior, continually discounting herself. When those two were "married" and driving her, she appeared to be in grave danger. The image of the play that she herself had written became a continuing one that she could use whenever she caught herself in the hateful-discounting pattern of thought. It was also true that the couple in the front seat of her life reflected the patterns she was taught as she grew up. Since the culture of her home town said that the way a woman could be successful was to attract men, have a "good" marriage (usually with social and economic overtones), and keep a house, she was by those standards the failure she felt herself to be in her depression. Intellectually she had rejected those values, but they nestled deep within her, preventing her from seeing the genuine worth of her accomplishments. With the help of this dream, she could begin to see that she was being successful in other ways than the traditional ones of her childhood home.

When the animus function is not consciously related to, a woman can become "possessed" by increasingly angry and negative animus behavior, which can cause her to be "opinionated, argumentative, rigid, controlling, and excessively critical of herself or others."[1] Such possession can be recognized by the stridency and absolutism of the woman's opinions, which brook no disagreement. As indicated, these opinions can be destructively directed toward her own abilities and value, paralyzing her ability to live life fully. The conversation of such a possessed woman is full of such words as "should," "ought," "always," and "never." The negative animus allows no exceptions.

Such negative animus opinions can also be projected onto other people, especially men, in which case it seems to the woman that "they" believe her to be worthless and incapable of valuable achievements. As with all projections, it takes a lot of work with her animus for a woman to withdraw the projection and own, as the woman above did, that she herself is "writing that play."

By the same token, of course, the positive animus can be projected onto a man. Then, as we noted in the chapter on the anima, the woman experiences great love or admiration for the man on whom the projection has occurred. Even though the symbolic significance is very positive in such cases, it is just as hard for a woman to own her own positive animus as it is to own the negative.

When a woman has worked with her animus enough to have stopped some of the possession and projections, she begins to encounter increasingly numinous aspects of the positive potential in herself. She also can begin to experience the deeper aspect of the animus as her archetypal psychopomp, her inner guide to the spirit, a mediator between consciousness and the deeper potential within. Sometimes the language is quite specific, as when one unknown man announced to a woman in her dream, "I am your guide to lead you through the trackless wastes of the Sierra Leones." At other times, though not so clearly announced, they seem to be luring her toward a mysterious and fearful unknown territory.

Such a dream came to a young woman of thirty-two after she had been in analysis for a year and a half, working on various family issues—her feelings of inadequacy as the mother of her small child and of lack of communication and support from her husband:

> I dreamed that I went on a sojourn or pilgrimage with a tall, dark man. We went up into the mountains.
>
> Then we were in an underground grotto. We were to go swimming in a huge underground lake or river. The water was very clear. I sat or stood at the edge and could see all sorts of fish swimming around in the water. My partner was swimming with the fish, but I was a little bit afraid and sat on the bank.
>
> I felt like I had been in this place before, dreamt this dream before.

The dream felt special for the dreamer, who described it as having a peaceful, nice feeling. She was not a religious person, yet she associated (with a little embarrassment) religious words with the dream. They were not words she usually used: sojourn, pilgrimage, grotto. The first two she associated with a search for self-knowledge, as sacred. Mountains were quiet, peaceful, an escape from everyday life. The grotto itself was quiet, peaceful, dark, and holy.

Like many modern young people, she had previously sought to find her meaning in relationships, which kept erupting in turmoil, and in drugs, which gave her only temporary relief from a sense of the meaninglessness of life. Her outer situation had improved, but this dream points her toward a deeper plunge—into the clear water of her depths, inside the mountain, where the living fish are swimming. She is still a little afraid, but the positive animus swims, staying with her and encouraging her. The search for what this means specifically in each life is an individual search, but this dream became for the young woman a place she could go in her memory to find peace and strength from the continuing turmoil. Thus she was one step on the road toward relating to the inner guide. These images carried their own energy to enable her to go the next steps on her way.

Such work allows the animus to begin to serve his appropriate function in her individuation process, that of a mediator or bridge to her relationship with the Self, the archetype of wholeness.

•12

Snakes

To come to a new awareness is usually a challenge. When a person is ready for it, a new insight may be greeted with enthusiasm; however, even when the time has come for a new development, one is not always aware of that fact, not to mention being ready to welcome it. The unknown is usually rather frightening. When you have learned to get around so well by crawling, why try to walk, when it seems very likely you will fall down? On the other hand, curiosity, the desire to be effective, the desire for competence (not to mention the sex and power drives), all pull one into life—all pull one into undertaking the "hero journey."

Spiritual growth or development, as well as ideas on the conscious level, are frequently symbolized in dreams by birds of one kind or another. Birds are associated with the wind and with the ability to fly up and away—to "transcend" the earthly plane. Creatures that live in the depths of nature are commonly symbolic of something in the unconscious. Snakes, lizards, rodents, and sometimes fish represent a piece of life that is underground or underwater, below the level of consciousness. Wild ducks and swans are intermediate, mostly on the surface, but able to move into the air and, to some extent, underwater. Jung wrote, "The lower vertebrates have from earliest times been favorite symbols of the collective psychic substratum which is localized anatomically in the subcortical centres, the cerebellum and the spinal cord. These organs constitute the snake. Snake-dreams usually occur, therefore, when the conscious mind is deviating from its instinctual basis."[1] The possible symbols for the challenge of new awareness are probably as numerous as the number of dreamers. However, we have been fascinated by one particular symbol—the snake—which seems to present the challenge to integrate our instinctual base with some new level of consciousness. Jung said, "The idea of transformation and renewal by means of a serpent is a well-substantiated archetype."[2]

From earliest times, the snake has been an impressive symbol for people in quite different parts of the world. The snake figures prominently, for example, in the Australian aborigines' story of creation. Everywhere it represents power; it can, of course, be a deadly danger. In folk stories, magic pools are generally guarded by snakes, just as serpents or dragons guard treasure of all kinds. The snake's chthonic nature, being close to the earth and cold blooded, is partly responsible for its mystery and fascination. By the fact that it shed its skin and kept living, it seems to have suggested to the earliest people that it was immortal and could live forever or could heal itself. In ancient Greece, in the rites and temples of the healing god, Asklepios, snakes were said to be encountered "at every step."[3] The healing quality associated with the snake has provided the medical profession with a logo. As it is seen today, coiled around the staff of the healing god, it seems to embody a kind of mediation between earth and heaven. In certain yogic practices in India the goal of spiritual development is understood as raising the kundalini, the serpent, or "serpent power," through the chakras (spiritual centers in the body) from the base of the spine to the head. For the person who experiences this, there is a healing or resolution of the duality that constitutes the phenomenal world; oneness with the cosmos is achieved.

One of the most common associations in the Western world is the Garden of Eden story in the Bible where the snake is associated with the coming to consciousness of the first humans. In the story it is the snake who tells Eve that eating of the forbidden fruit of the tree of the knowledge of good and evil will make one wise. Eating is, of course, a symbol of taking something in, of incorporating it. The knowledge of good and evil is the awareness of two opposing possibilities, which is the essence of consciousness. For some people, to come to a new awareness feels like disobedience, for the comfort and security of the past has been left behind; they are no longer being true to what they know works. Furthermore, they cannot go back; the "poison" of the new prevents it.

One can never say what a dream symbol means apart from the dreamer's personal associations, but there are some common motifs that occur in the dreams of a great many people. The snake is one such rich symbol, having been a part, often a dangerous part, of the human experience from earliest times. The symbol of the snake goes so deep that, as D.H. Lawrence said, "a rustle in the grass can startle the toughest 'modern' to depths he has no control over."[4] Snakes are both fascinating and frightening. This combination of attraction and fear is the mark of the numinous. Jungian analyst Edward Whitmont says, "The attraction-fear combination marks the call from the transpersonal Self; it also signals the need for the ego personality to translate such calls into a viable and acceptable form of expression."[5] Snake dreams often seem to suggest that a person is being presented with a new possibility—the transformation of an old attitude or way of being.

Even without any personal amplification from the dreamer's life situation the following snake dream of a forty-four-year-old woman illustrates the compensatory relationship between consciousness and the unconscious:

> I dreamed about a huge or large black snake which was very gentle, almost smiling. I was not afraid of it and picked it up. The snake seemed to have a sense of humor.

The dream seems to be saying either: "you are taking some matter too seriously" (as the snake has a sense of humor and is smiling), or, "you are taking a serious matter (a huge black snake) too lightly, as if a snake had a sense of humor or could smile at you." Just what the matter is of which the dreamer is unaware is not revealed in the dream—the dreamer would have to relate that to her life situation.

In a dream the threat of a snake bite may well be pointing to the threat of being "bitten" with a new awareness. Wallace had not been in Zurich long and underway with his analysis when he had a dream in which all his family-of-origin were gathered with him in the comfort of a backyard patio. He was sitting near an ivy-covered brick wall and suddenly realized, out of the corner of his eye, that a snake was very close and eyeing him. He jumped to avoid it and woke up. Obviously it was a time when Wallace was being presented with the possibility of an increase in consciousness. There is a kind of comfort, like a "backyard patio," about the attitudes with which one has been brought up. To leave them is a little frightening. The historian of religions C. Kerenyi says that ivy and snake symbolism have a close association in Greek religion, and both are particularly associated with Dionysos.[6] At least since the time of Nietzsche, Dionysos has been associated with the mystery of the "other," the unknown and that which is antagonistic to prevailing cultural attitudes. Dionysos is thus symbolic of another kind of awareness—perhaps of the unconscious and all that it might contain.

A few weeks later Wallace dreamed that he was swimming in the backyard of his family home (there was actually no swimming pool there), and a friendly snapping turtle kept nibbling at his legs. It was a pleasant experience, and he wasn't frightened. In fact, in the dream the turtle smiled at Wallace. Water is often symbolic of the unconscious, and this dream seems to present a "snapshot" of the situation at the time: Wallace had become more at home in the exploration of the unconscious, even with reference to childhood attitudes, and experienced his new awareness with pleasure. He doesn't mind being "nibbled." The turtle is not a snake, but is a member of the reptile family that is at home in the water. The turtle also had other associations for Wallace from his time in the Far East: with wisdom, and with the ancestor tablets (records of deeds) of kings which were mounted on turtle backs. Wallace's past history was being held up for examination through unconscious material.

Dreams present a picture of one's situation; however, there is still a choice. One can choose to stay with the understanding already achieved. The following dream suggests a situation in which the unconscious of a young girl holds up the possibility of an increase in consciousness, but says, in effect, "so far, you are dropping it." She was in her first or second year of college but was there perhaps more for the social life and to satisfy parents than to learn new ideas. She took a course in dream analysis, probably just for the "fun" of it, during which time she dreamed:

> I am home, but outside, and I am looking over this railing, looking down in a stairway. There are snakes there. A man reaches down and is bringing them on up to us. An old girl friend is there with me. He is handing them to us; I won't take any. I am scared of them. There was a big snake, an egg-swallower, and a small one. We are supposed to do something with it. We went in the kitchen and started to look at a magazine on the table. The girl friend told me to hold the snake. I would not. She handed it over to me, but I did not reach out to get it and it dropped on the floor with a thud.

The dream seems to be saying: from your home place (the attitudes of childhood) you are looking down a stairway (looking inside?); an unknown man (animus figure) that is a part of you is presenting you with a possibility of new awareness (snakes), which is scary. You are "supposed to do something with it" (the choice is up to you); but you keep giving your attention to conventional ideas (the magazine). A part of you (the old girl friend, a positive shadow figure?) tells you to go forward with the new development, but you refuse, and the possibility drops with a thud. The big snake, the "egg-swallower" is an interesting feature in the dream. As eggs are that out of which new life comes, there is even an additional suggestion of new possibility in the egg symbolism. Also, the fact that they are in a "kitchen"—a place of transformation, where the raw is turned into the cooked—is indicative of the basic motif.

A professional woman in her early thirties also dreamed of snakes in the kitchen. She was divorced, had two children, and had just decided firmly to break off a relationship with a man and work on a graduate degree full time while maintaining job and home. While making these decisions, she also decided to get more in touch with her unconscious. This dream might be called "Guess Who's Coming to Dinner":

> I reached for a box of noodles on top of the refrigerator and found a bunch of snakes living in the box. I knew I had to get rid of them. I went for help to a place that seemed like a school—or at least the place in which I found myself was a school corridor. There was a man there who gave some advice but it was somehow clear this was a job I had to do myself. He seemed slightly amused.
>
> I emptied the snakes out of the box. They were very quick and very strong. I grabbed the head of the one that seemed to be the leader, went into a place that seemed to be a janitorial closet and also may have been my kitchen. I filled a bucket of water and held its head under for a long time—that required a lot of strength as the snake was strong and wrestled with me. I began to feel bad, to feel I was doing the wrong thing.
>
> I lifted the snake out of the water. He was still alive and had two heads then. We conversed for a while. I realized the thing to do was make friends.
>
> In the next scene, the snake was sitting at my dining room table. The kids seemed to be there. The table was set nicely—put together as I do when someone special is coming to dinner. I still felt a little wary, but I was mostly amused and very curious about my company.

The setting (the kitchen) suggests a place of transformation. The first reaction of the dreamer is to get rid of these possibilities, and she goes for help to a "school"—a place where things are learned. An unknown man (animus) gives some advice, but she realizes she has to do the job herself. She has resistance to what is offered—she tries to drown the snake. The strength of the snake may indicate the power of the need for a new awareness. She begins to change her perspective, her decision. When she lifts the snake out, it has two heads. Jung says the appearance of two of a kind in dreams shows a duality or conflict. This doubling effect frequently suggests that something is close to consciousness, probably because of the tension created in the dreamer by the conflict. There is even a saying, "two heads are better than one." She enters into dialogue with the new awareness and realizes that "the thing to do was make friends."

This dream reviews the situation and describes the change in attitude that the dreamer had undertaken, but it calls to her attention that she has foolishly tried to drown a snake (hold it in the unconscious) instead of befriending it. By its whimsical ending, the dream lures her into friendship with her snake of new awareness.

Still another dream of a snake in a kitchen is the following which occurred for the dreamer at a time of transition and coming to terms with a new understanding:

> I was in my kitchen and there was a large tiger snake. It reared up, balancing on its coils, in order to sniff noses in greeting (the way my little cat does with my ex-husband and my son). It came to greet me. I was frightened but stood my ground. We sniffed noses and then it slithered out my cat door.

At the time of this dream the dreamer was forty-one and becoming deeply involved with a much younger man who tragically died in a car accident two months later. Looking back two years later, the dreamer said: "That relationship brought me in touch with my feminine self and led me to recognize that I was not suited to the academic life." In view of the dreamer's comment, it is interesting to look at the motif of the cat, which is often associated with the feminine. The dreamer is challenged to meet the snake (awareness of the conflict she felt between academic life and her feminine nature) with the same affectionate response which the two men in her life made to her cat. Her particular snake, a *tiger* snake, in its name as well as its behavior, is associated with the cat and thus the feminine.

A therapist, late in her life, gave us the following dream which she had many years earlier at a crucial time of change. Early in life she had been a teacher but became a psychotherapist working with adults and children on two continents. She had treasured this numinous dream for years:

> I was lying on the ground, flat on my back. From the right, a snake was approaching. Then it was passing over my forehead. I was afraid. Then a voice said, "Be still. The serpent power is within you. The snake will not harm you." I shuddered. Then I was still. The snake passed on its way.

The dreamer was, at the time, unaware of any such phrases as "serpent power" (as in Kundalini Yoga) or of the symbolism of the snake. Yet the power of the dream had always remained a living reality to her.

The dreamer in the next dream spent a year of professional training in Denver with a diverse group of skilled leaders gathered from different areas. Some months after returning home she dreamed:

> A small old-fashioned house fairly dimly lit. I wasn't aware of any windows. Two friends were with me in the house, Jack and Jane. I was standing in the doorway between two rooms when I noticed a small thick snake, a death adder, in the next room where Jack was. I was afraid to go in the room but Jane encouraged me to. Jack offered to put the snake outside for me but it turned out to be a toy snake. Jane held it up by the tail and it moved about.

Jack was a friend from the stimulating group that she had studied with in Denver. Jane was a friend and colleague at her home. The dreamer said that at the time of the dream she was struggling with the transition between returning to her work at home and the study in Denver with the group of new friends with whom she had shared exciting ideas and developed close bonds. She said, "I remember waking up—with a powerful sense that the separation had been healed within me and I had finally returned home." The dream pictures the situation graphically. There has not been a lot of consciousness about integrating her new insights into her work at home; the setting of the dream is a "small old-fashioned house" that is "dimly lit." A house is where we live; she has been in an "old-fashioned" one and not very conscious. Light is symbolic of consciousness, as with the cartoonist light bulb above the head. She is frightened to be in the same room with the new possibilities (it looks like a "death adder"), but another part of her encourages her to enter the same room (where there is also an animus figure associated with her experiences in Denver). When she does, she finds it is not dangerous but rather something to play with—that only appears frightening at first sight.

The next dream is from a thirty-one-year-old married woman, with children, who had become dissatisfied with being "just a wife and mother," though her traditional ideas make her feel as if *all* her attention had to be there. In an attempt at independence, she had gone to India with a woman friend. An airline strike stranded them for several days in Hong Kong, and she experienced trauma from it, though the friend enjoyed the extra holiday. She felt helpless and out of control. Partly, the fear seemed to come from being away from the children longer than the arrangements she had made for them—even though they were with their father. After her return home she had this dream the night after she had telephoned to make an appointment for her first therapy hour:

> My husband and I were in India at a meeting with lots of women about how much something had helped them. They were supposed to create clothes, and they all looked terrible in their outfits. When it was over, he and I had trouble leaving. The hall was too crowded, wrong instructions, and then we ended up in a stream full of ducks. We were waist-deep in the dirty, filthy, mushy water and surrounded by so many big ducks it was impossible to move. I tried to push and kick the ducks away.
>
> Then we were at this nice Indian hotel, and people were gathered in small groups talking and drinking and relaxing in a large lobby with many rooms opening into each other. There was a snake in every room, usually on the tile floor, and Indian music. I kept looking out for the snakes. My husband and I sat on a sofa, and he was all relaxed. I looked behind me, and there was a snake on the cushion. I yelled and jumped up, and just then another snake in my sock bit me. It hurt terribly, and I pulled off my sock, and the snake wouldn't let go, and I banged my foot against the floor, but the snake never let go. It hurt so bad. The snake bit me in the middle of the soul [sic] of my right foot. My husband was not

quick to help, and he just stayed lying on the sofa. I said we should not have come here.

As we have said, "initial dreams" are often indicative of the direction and concerns that will be presented in the course of the analysis. Only a few aspects of this significant dream will be mentioned here.

The opening sentences suggest the general setting: the attempt at independence (going to India) and the persona problem ("supposed to create clothes" but they look terrible). The ducks are birds that can fly (symbolic of the spirit) but also that are able to "duck under" water (into the unconscious). The dream suggests that the dreamer will get "waist-deep" in some "dirty, filthy, mushy" stuff but with lots of big possibilities (actually, too many ducks to be able to move).

Then the scene changes in the dream to describe another aspect. A hotel is a more "collective" symbol, where a lot of people are, as opposed to one's own house. There are lots of possibilities there— "with many rooms opening into each other." There is a snake, however, in every room, and it is frightening. The "husband" in the dream needs to be considered both on the objective level (as her actual husband) and the subjective level (as an inner animus figure). He is not concerned about the "dangers" (the snakes), but the dream ego thinks maybe they "should not have come here." The dreamer would probably say it was a thoughtless spelling error, made while sleepy, to have written "soul of my right foot" instead of sole; however, such "slips" have significance if Freud was right. This new possibility has bitten her "in the middle of her soul," and it will not let go. What will she do about it? The initial dream seems to have described the challenge which she faces.

The following dream was given us by a forty-two-year-old man who said it came soon after he started recording his dreams some three or four years earlier:

> I am traveling down a dark road at night. To my left is a house with an abundance of trees and plants. I move toward the house and hear music. I see one lighted window. I enter and find myself on a "patio" or in an enclosed garden. I move closer to the window. The feeling I have as I approach is fear of the unknown. It feels like the end of summer. The music is the theme from the Archie Bunker TV program. I follow the music and see a black man through the window. He is about thirty or thiry-five years old,

very dark and rather large. He seems to be watching the TV. I ask him through the open window if there is a rest room there. He directs me through the patio through a door or passage leading outside. I go to the side of the building and urinate on the ground. He joins me and we are both facing a dark wood and are urinating against a dirt bank. The urine is turning into a snake. This is a frightening experience. My apprehension is intensifying. I look toward the black man and see he is offering me a bird held on his hand. The bird is small and gray, brownish. He gestures for me to take it from his finger and tells me I *must* chant certain words to the bird each day. This seems very important and I am further terrified. I think I will never be able to remember the words of the chant. However, it became simpler and I then believe I can remember and I reach for the bird.

The setting of the dream is reminiscent of the opening lines of Dante's *Divine Comedy*, for the dreamer, in "the middle of the journey of life" loses his way and finds himself facing a "dark wood." The dreamer says he grew up in "Archie Bunker country," though he never held those values. The black man is a shadow figure, appropriately a few years younger than the dreamer. Urinating seems to be symbolically associated with spontaneity. The snake comes about as a result of the *joint* urinating of the dreamer and the black man. The dreamer found the experience frightening and looked to the shadow figure who offered him a bird (a new spirit?), but told him he had to give it some attention each day. The dreamer was afraid he would not be able to remember, but then he decided it was simpler than he thought and reached for the bird. The dream ends on this positive note, having described both the setting in the dreamer's life at the time and the positive direction his inner development could take. This becomes clear in the dreamer's reflections on his situation at the time of the dream:

Something new began to happen to me about three or four years ago. I had just moved from one part of my state to another. The change was welcomed and I now found myself only 25 miles from the city where I was born. I was slowly beginning to feel like a new person. I experienced life and myself in a very positive light, much more confident and possessing a strong sense of well-being. I felt freer and at times very alive and joyful. Tears seemed to come easy but were, in a sense, joyful tears. I now find myself easily stirred, especially when I hear of or experience something to do with harmony or communion or brotherhood. I remember really sobbing when I saw the video tape of the M. L. King speech "I have a dream." For the most part these were new feelings and experiences for me or, at the very least, were much larger now. For the first time I experienced myself as gifted. I had many memories of pain in childhood and in my youth, but somehow despite this, I had come through it all and with some wholeness and joy. For this I feel deeply grateful and see this simply as a gift of grace.

This dream seems to herald the challenge of new awareness, and the dreamer's later reflections confirm that it was a challenge met and integrated.

We are indebted to Diana Neutze of Melbourne, Australia, for calling our attention to a literary example of the transformation which can come from welcoming the snake. In *The Rime of the Ancient Mariner*, while the Mariner lives in torment for having killed the Albatross, who had brought the winds to his becalmed ship, he views the sea serpents as "slimy things . . . Upon the slimy sea." His companions have hung the Albatross, like a cross, about his neck, and cursing him, they have all died. In the midst of his appalling despair and suffering, he perceives the beauty of the water-snakes and reports, "A spring of love gushed from my heart,/And I blessed them unaware." The transformation of his consciousness began at that moment: "The self-same moment I could pray;/And from my neck so free/The Albatross fell off, and sank/Like lead into the sea." His fate changes with the spring of love for the snakes in appreciation for their beauty, and this represents for him the beauty of all of creation. In his new consciousness, he wanders the world telling his story and urging on everyone he meets the love of all things "great and small." He has met the challenge of new awareness, and this awareness is integrated into a transcendent, reconciling symbol of love.

• 13

The Trickster

The archetype of the trickster is a parallel figure to the individual shadow. The trickster is a sort of collective shadow figure, a summation of all the inferior or unrecognized traits of character in individuals. Jung characterizes the trickster as the archetypal aspect of the shadow. However, it soon becomes apparent when working with tricksters that they do not follow the gender patterns of the shadow; sometimes women have male tricksters and men have female tricksters, though male tricksters are more common for both sexes.

The very name "trickster" leads to the main way they can be spotted—they play tricks. "Fate playing tricks" is a common experience, and Freudian slips are a form of such tricks from the unconscious—where one mis-states or mis-hears, loses things or forgets things—usually at what seems "the worst possible time." Jung's archetypal studies of trickster figures illuminate the meaning of these personal tricksters.

The organizing archetype "trickster" is behind fools, jesters, clowns, satyrs, scapegoats, devils, the god Pan, and a myriad of other images of folly. The trickster has been observed in myth-cycles of all peoples, in medieval religious carnivals involving the reversal of hierarchic order (still observable in some carnival festivities today), in classical and alchemical figures such as Hermes/Mercurius, in folk fairy tales, and in comedy routines throughout history.

Jung has identified a number of typical trickster motifs and traits, such as a fondness for sly jokes and malicious pranks, power as a shape-shifter, a dual nature (half animal, half divine), and exposure to all kinds of tortures. The trickster has a low level of intelligence and his "communications" tend to be fatuous. He reduces the world around him to chaos. He frequently plays malicious jokes on people only to fall victim in his turn to the vengeance of those whom he has injured, thus sometimes being in peril of his life. His behavior is unpredictable, with senseless orgies of destruction and self-imposed suffering.

Jung thinks the trickster motif is extremely ancient, "haunting" the mythology of all ages, in "picaresque tales, in carnivals and revels, in magic rites of healing, in man's religious fears and exaltations . . . ."[1] From all of this he thinks the trickster is a "psychologem," an archetypal structure of extreme antiquity, originating in a psyche that has hardly left the animal level. The historical source of the trickster is, then, as "a faithful reflection of absolutely undifferentiated human consciousness."

In probing the meaning of an archetype, though, Jung says one can never look only at the historical sources but must also look to the *function* of the archetype. What can be the purpose or meaning of this crude primitivity in modern lives? Jung says the trickster forms a picture of a much earlier level of development, being dragged along in modern times as a senseless appendage, but that his presence, felt on the highest levels of civilization, indicates the trickster is more than a historical remnant. Mere vestiges of an early state that is dying usually lose their energy and disappear. Since the trickster remains, it evidently serves a purpose now.

The historical approach has shown that in the trickster a higher level of consciousness has covered up a lower one. Jung asks the question: what happens to these lower qualities when people become more civilized? He answers that they have not "gone up in smoke" but have merely withdrawn into the unconscious. Until consciousness finds itself in a critical or doubtful situation, they wait there, looking for a favorable opportunity to reappear as a projection on a neighbor. Jung sees a great threat to civilization in having forgotten the danger of the trickster:

> The so-called civilized man has forgotten the trickster. He remembers him only figuratively and metaphorically, when, irritated by his own ineptitude, he speaks of fate playing tricks on him or of things being bewitched. He never suspects that his own hidden and apparently harmless shadow has qualities whose dangerousness exceeds his wildest dreams. As soon as people get together in masses and submerge the individual, the shadow is mobilized, and, as history shows, may even be personified and incarnated.[2]

Jung says that when the dangerous shadow is ignored or forgotten, then people fall into the error (Jung calls it "puerility") of thinking that they themselves are in perfect order and that only their material deprivation is the problem—that the meaning of existence lies in food, clothing, and the possession of an automobile. As a result, the individual loses the capacity for introspection and relies on the external environment. A personal code of ethics is replaced by laws, leaving, for example, soldiers who never subject orders which they receive from superiors to ethical scrutiny. Jung says an individual in such a condition "has not yet made the discovery that he might be capable of spontaneous ethical impulses, and of performing them—even when no one is looking." This leads Jung to the meaning and purpose of the trickster myth:

> From this point of view we can see why the myth of the trickster was preserved and developed: like many other myths, it was supposed to have a therapeutic effect. It holds the earlier low intellectual and moral level before the eyes of the more highly developed individual, so that he shall not forget how things looked yesterday.[3]

The trickster figure, by the very tricks he plays, points to potential disaster, which in itself is an increase in consciousness. The trickster raises the problems and asks the questions and will not allow them to be ignored. He is thus the first step toward finding solutions and answers.

Furthermore, the trickster contains important values, "hiding meaningful contents under an unprepossessing exterior." Consciousness itself has been portrayed as having been wrested by various mythological tricksters, such as Prometheus, who stole fire from the gods. The charming south Pacific trickster Maui used tricks to fish up an island from the sea as well as to get the secret of fire. He even tricked the sun itself and failed only when he tried to capture the secret of immortality.

Initiation rites have used trickster motifs as if to demonstrate that increasing maturity requires liberation from "any state of being that is too immature, too fixed or final." Tricksters at the highest level of maturity have moved beyond mere magical tricks-of-the-trade to reveal the true spiritual insights of shamans or master yogis.[4]

The very purpose of transforming the meaningless into the meaningful reveals to Jung the trickster's compensatory relation to the "saint" and "approximation to the saviour." This transformation operates through an inversion of the meaningful and meaningless, the kind of action based on the ancient saturnalia. During the annual festival of the Roman god Saturn, all business was at a standstill, schools were closed, executions and military operations did not take place (!), and slaves were temporarily freed, feasting with and even waited on by their masters and saying what they chose. The whole Roman value system was mocked by this holiday and nothing was sacred. The basic formula of this saturnalian pattern of inversion has been seen as: "through release to clarification."[5] The vitality which was normally locked up in order was released in the festivity.

The clarification in this release comes from a heightened awareness of the relation between human beings and nature. This involves a mockery of what is unnatural, and a complementary mockery of what is merely natural, which puts both in the perspective of life as a whole. Both sides are important. The kill-joys are not capable of pleasure, and the inadequately developed people are unable to know when the revel should end. Thus not only hostility to pleasure is mocked, but highflown idealism is mocked, too, as an attempt to be too "high and mighty."

The other side of trickster misrule is that he implies a rule; he is part of human nature, but only a part. Clowning can help to set limits by going beyond the limits. The trickster figures thus are images which can serve as a healing force for a view of life that is too high, too pure, and overheroic. When the unconsciousness which the trickster typifies is brought to the light of consciousness, then humankind is seen more truly.

Another way to see this relationship is to note the curious interplay in myths and dreams between trickster motifs and hero motifs. We have already noted that hero images tend to appear when the ego needs strengthening. Dreamers sometimes perceive that when they are feeling afraid to move forward or take risks a hero appears. On the other hand, when they take their own heroic stance a trifle too seriously or absolutely, some trickster image or moment appears.

Who does not know the experience of falling flat on your face just when you wanted to look the best or perhaps spilling red sauce down the front of the shirt or blouse donned fastidiously for being seated at the head table. On solemn visits of the bishop, a falling ceiling tile can send small altar boys into uncontrollable giggles which the congregation is too full of propriety to join in. All these experiences look toward achieving a balanced view of life. Charlie Chaplin's little clown makes everyone laugh, and some of the laughter is to keep from crying. Archie Bunker's clownish excesses have probably converted more people to tolerance than all the sermons in the country. Thus can the tricksters save.

A detailed examination of one of Jean's dreams and the life situation in which it occurred will illustrate further what can be learned from such dreams—and how hard it can be to acknowledge tricksters:

> There was to be a witnessing meeting and a girl had agreed to witness. A large group of rather rough-looking people came in with her husband. The meeting had been proceeding; and when she stood up to speak, her husband began to cackle like a chicken. He kept on and on quite loudly. Finally, about three young men, who were also tough-looking, arose and quietly took him out. I remember looking at him as he left and wondering why anyone would act like that. I thought he might be "off" mentally.

The dream continues with further, similar interruptions. Jean's personal associations with witnesssing meetings were from the parish church where we were confirmed. On Sunday evenings, as the outreach of evangelism, different lay people would "witness," that is, tell their story of the difference faith in God made in their daily lives. We had been active in these meetings for several years, and we had felt (and still do feel) that this is one of the most effective ways to get in touch with the reality of a living God who acts in ordinary people's lives. So Jean had a lot of strong feeling tied up in such meetings.

At the same time, you will recall from the dreams in the animus chapter, Jean was nervous about whether this psychology was a danger to the faith she had found as an adult and which was such a treasure for her. She feared (probably quite accurately) that her analyst at the time was skeptical of her faith, which made it hard to hear his interpretation of this dream with an open mind. He suggested that witnessing meetings sometimes lacked humor and that some witnesses were even hypocrites. Jean coldly rejected all such suggestions. The analytical hour was a debate, a jockeying, a stand-off, with Jean's defensiveness foremost in her focus. Finally, the analyst referred her to some reading about tricksters.

It is clear at first reading that the witnessing girl's husband is a trickster; his actions have that kind of mindless absurdity in the midst of a serious occasion which is the trickster's trademark. Only years later (and no longer afraid of the challenges to her church) could Jean begin to see the humor in the dream, though honesty always forbade her denying that, after all, *her* unconscious had produced the dream. Why did her unconscious produce the dream at that time? This is always a good question to ask.

The answer seems to be that the trickster came to show Jean that her attitude toward witnessing was too serious, too "high and mighty." It was hard for her to face up to this. Part of her defensiveness came from looking at the dream with an either-or attitude. Jean felt that *either* witnessing was all good *or* her faith was nothing. The trickster, who constellates—absurdly—a criticism of the possibilities inherent in going too far with anything, can help one detect such a lack of balance. People who witness in churches *may*, after all, be insincere or phony, just as people anywhere may be. Jean's absolute and unquestioning defense of all witnessing was not in balance. As tricksters never know when the revel should end, dreamers need to maintain their conscious point of view. However, they also need to be unafraid to question their attitudes about the most important aspects of their lives.

The historical figure who probably exemplifies this more than any other is St. Francis of Assisi. G.K. Chesterton emphasizes this side of Francis by pointing to his actions as having "a freedom almost amounting to frivolity," to his having an "inverted vision," becoming almost a "symbol of inversion," and having a particular vocation to "astonish and awaken the world." This vocation sounds like what the trickster can do—astonish and awaken. Francis carried out this vocation, Chesterton suggests, by a sort of antithesis: "the act is always unexpected and never inappropriate."[6] The world was so inverted that the kind of reversal Francis pointed to was appropriate to show the world what it needed to see.

This vocation to astonish and awaken showed up in Francis very early in his religious life. Francis, feeling called by a vision to repair God's house, sold some of the cloth which his father, a cloth merchant, had left with him, took the money and gave it to the priest of the church where his vision occurred. The priest, by the way, thought at first Francis was playing some kind of practical joke on him. Hauled before the bishop of the ecclesiastical court by his father, Francis, having been told that all he had came from his father, stripped his clothes off and returned them, leaving himself naked—except for a hair shirt!

It is also reported that as people asked him to pray for them, he would drop to his knees in the middle of the road and begin praying aloud for the person. Imagine the embarrassed glancing from side to side by the unwary requester, the desire to say, "No, no, I didn't mean now—like this!"

His whole life was lived at that unexpected level. This was true also on the very serious plane. He himself attributed his "conversion" (itself a turning around to the opposite) to the time when he brought himself to embrace a leper, the outcasts of society who had formerly evoked from him the extremity of disgust, with their terrible sores, mutilated bodies, and awful smell. Chesterton says this is how his entire, world-changing ministry was carried out:

> There is in it something of gentle mockery of the very idea of possessions; something of a hope of disarming the enemy by generosity; something of a humorous sense of bewildering the worldly with the unexpected; something of the joy of carrying an enthusiastic conviction to a logical extreme.[7]

The much-beloved prayer of St. Francis has this same rhythm of opposition: "where there is hatred, let me sow love"; with the results spelled out as well—"for it is in pardoning that we are pardoned." Something very close to the nature of the rhythm of life itself is touched by this kind of trickster understanding. It is the pattern of the beatitudes: "blessed are those who mourn, for they shall be comforted."

The trickster moments always contain the seed of conversion to their opposite; yet they do not prescribe absolutely what to do. That is still a personal decision. Sometimes fervently held collective views need to be swept away. The most serious and devoted religious people of Jesus' day were so devoted to the law that they didn't want anyone healed on the Sabbath because it was the day of rest. It does not deny the need to keep the Sabbath holy to see that it is good to heal people then as well. Healing is a higher holiness; it is a sense of perspective, which sees that the person needing to be healed is more important than the rule.

Ignored, tricksters, like shadow figures of all kinds, may turn more and more serious. Hamlet, whose uncertainties toss him first one way and then the other, plays tricks that grow increasingly serious as he moves through the play. He begins so nobly, but later almost maniacally kills people right and left as part of his plan to avenge a killing. He becomes what he avenges, partly by his unconsciousness.

Hitler himself, portrayed so amusingly by Chaplin, became for the whole world the embodiment of all the worst that is hidden in humanity. The world still tries to understand how such a holocaust could come to be in one of the most educated areas of the world. Hitler was treated as a joke at first, but in him the archetype got out of hand and captured hordes of others, who lost all sense of perspective about human life and goals. Only when people find within themselves the tricksters which they are capable of acting out can there be an end to such events as carnival revelers dressed in clown costumes made from bloody Torah pages.

It may be that this ancient psychologem of trickster is itself the archetype of the tendency of something to change into its opposite— suddenly to become that which is its antithesis. If so, then no true wisdom is possible without the knowledge of this possibility. Jung cites Heraclitus as discovering this "marvelous psychological law," called *enantiodromia*—the regulative function of the opposites. Jung says our rational attitude of culture is always in danger of running into its opposite, the irrational devastation of culture. Consciousness which operates in full knowledge of the grim possibilities in the unconscious instead of repressing them is the only escape from being torn asunder by the opposites.[8] The symbolic process is an experience of images which have an enantiodromian structure and present a rhythm of negative and positive, loss and gain, dark and light.[9] Eastern philosophy understands this cyclic rhythm as the West has often failed to do. The terms and the symbol of yin and yang portray this balanced principle, with the seed of light in the darkness and the seed of darkness in the light. There seems to exist an optimum in all of nature, which, when exceeded, produces an enantiodromia.[10] It may be that this is nature's process of change and growth, and thus of life. Such a trickster force enables the warring halves of the personality to reunite and brings the civil war to an end. The trickster may then be perceived as one of the truest and deepest motifs of transformation.

•14

Death and Rebirth

Death and rebirth as a motif of transformation is as obvious as nature (the death and rebirth of vegetation; sunset, sunrise) and as subtle as the intricacies of meditation. That the old must be destroyed before the new can be born is a theme running deep not only in nature but also in human history. When the opposites get too far apart, death and rebirth form a uniting symbol. That the king must die in order for the nation or tribe to be renewed is a widespread mythological theme. In every life there are trials and tribulations of one kind or another. Death and rebirth is indeed, as we have noted earlier, one of the patterns often found in the "hero journey" of life. As psychiatrist M. Scott Peck has pointed out in *The Road Less Traveled,* in order to learn something new one must experience a death of the old self and its outworn perspective.[1] Initiation rites, from ancient times and in most cultures, have entailed a form of ritual death and the entrance into a new life. In Christianity, the theme is given a spiritual meaning: except you be born again, you cannot see the kingdom of God. The Christian initiation rite, baptism, is described as a death of the old person and a putting on of the new—symbolically represented by some Christians by total immersion, a ritual "drowning" and rising to a new life. Even in the secular world, New Year's Eve celebrations, when carried to excess, have a certain destructive quality about them as if that were necessary before the next day's New Year's resolutions could herald the new beginning.

Dreams of dying or of killing someone else are rather common motifs in dreams. Often, they have a nightmare quality, yet dreams of death do not usually refer to actual death. Understood on the subjective level, they can be seen to concern the death of attitudes or ways of approaching life—other people in the dream simply representing aspects of oneself, unknown qualities or ways of being. If the figure dying is associated with the past, then the dream may suggest an old part of oneself may be dying. If the figure is associated with an undeveloped potential, the dream can be a warning that one possible aspect of wholeness is being killed. Thus interpreted, nightmares may lose their terror, but not necessarily their pain—the "death" may still be hard to face.

The dreamer in the following dream was a thirty-three-year-old businessman who felt he was making no progress in the business world. He worried over the question: if he didn't work harder, was he stealing from his family? He loved them, but hated spending his whole life and energy just making more money. Then he had this dream:

> I'm living in a time of few people—either long ago or in the future. Life is simple. Something happens—some crime—maybe robbery. The penalty is death by drowning; I am the executioner. Six adults and four children are sentenced. The community is gathered on the banks of a wide, deep, slow-moving river. I am on one side with the community and the accused were in a line on the other bank. A rope was tied around each person, one at a time. I would hold the other end. They would enter the water, and I would drag and guide them through the depths of the water. There was little struggling; for the most part the adults accepted dying. But the thought kept eating at my head and heart that I'm taking a life. I was acting like God, or it was something only he should do. I was shaken and sickened by it. I felt trapped. When it came time for the kids, I asked them if they understood what was happening. They nodded yes, but they were scared and their innocence was so obvious (not innocence of the crime, but of life). I began to plead for them, "I can't do this; we can't do this. We have to make an exception or change things." I became emotional and awoke.

The people in the dream are unknown to him in his conscious life, which fact, along with the mythic setting, suggests that the dream should be viewed on the subjective level—all characters in the dream being aspects or potentialities of his. The dream says he is an executioner, carrying out orders to kill. He has killed some "adults," some older parts of himself; but when it comes time to kill the four children, he finds himself disheartened and unable to go forward with what he has been doing. It is not a matter of "crime" but of their "innocence of life" which stirs his emotions. He wants those potentialities (the children) to have a chance to live. For that to happen, the dream says, he has "to make an exception or change things."

A "near death" experience in a dream often reflects symbolically the intense emotional level of the life situation. A woman in her mid-thirties had this dream while she and her husband were working on difficulties in their marriage:

> I am in a small town with large trees and old houses. My husband, Fred, and I are looking at houses to buy. We look at five houses which are along the ridge with a view of the mountains and a large valley below them. One house is too small. One is a little tacky. One is like ours, and I would like to buy it, but Fred thinks it is too expensive. I am convinced that a house is so important that I should not settle for something I don't want, but Fred is not persuaded. I feel frustrated with him for being so narrow-minded.
>
> We are then walking through town and come to a swimming pool. I jump in and sink to the bottom and am floundering around. A beautiful, golden-haired young man comes over and pulls me up to the surface of the water where I can breathe again. Fred seems to be sitting along the side watching it all, and I wonder what it means.

The dreamer and her husband have not been able to figure out how to get a new house together (a house is symbolic of "where we live") and she "drowns" in despair. That is a picture of her situation (of which she was more or less aware) at the time of the dream, but in the dream a "golden-haired young man" comes to the rescue while the husband only sits there and watches. The figure of the husband in the dream can be viewed on both the objective level (the actual attitude of her husband) and the subjective level (an old animus side of herself). The dreamer, when asked about the rescuer in the dream, called him "an overidealized figure," which suggests she was having some difficulty in accepting the reality of a new possibility (a new animus orientation) within herself. Her old animus attitudes would evidently let her drown and be suspicious of any rescue. Can she learn to accept the new? The dream leaves it up to her.

A different kind of near death experience is reflected in the dream of a woman who had difficulty in accepting her feminity and her own uniqueness, which she associated with her Irish heritage. The dream focused on a green skirt which she linked with being Irish:

> There are only two of us—another woman and I—left in the world which is coming to an end. But someone tells me not to fear, but to continue to wear the skirt I have on. We might disintegrate, but will never die so long as I wear the green skirt. Then I said, "The skirt and all my clothes will be consumed in this stormy atmosphere." Then the voice said, "Not consumed but transformed. It—the clothes—will re-appear only to die and re-appear again."

The skirt in the dream was a particular skirt she owned—which she felt was "classy," unlike many of her clothes. She had realized that she moved differently when she wore skirts, but had always felt she did not look good in them. A strong introvert, she had difficulty letting her classy, natural, feminine self "out" in the world. She had entered therapy because of some troublesome changes in her life which gave her anxiety. The dreamer experienced the dream as assuring her that though her old world *was* coming to an end, she would not be destroyed. The dream encourages her acceptance of her own Irish and feminine being. The disembodied voice was important to her as she sought, despite the "stormy atmosphere," to bring to life those transformations.

Another dreamer experienced a strange "gift from the sea" (from the unconscious?):

> I dreamed I was talking to the mother of an early childhood friend. (She was my first and best friend from kindergarten until third grade, when my family and I moved to another town. I never saw her again.) I asked about her. The mother told me she had been dead for a long time, but she couldn't remember how it happened. We were on a beach and a casket washed up on the shore. The mother recognized it was my friend's casket, and she was distraught. I told her to open it and find out what was inside. She was very afraid, and I encouraged her. When she opened it, there was a picture of my friend and some of her belongings. The mother started to cry.

At the time of the dream the dreamer, a young woman, was dealing with a lot of loss, including the death of a parent and some other tragedies of close friends. The dream seems to go back to pick up her first great loss—of her young friend—and encourage her to look inside the "casket" where she is burying her pain currently. The dream was not frightening at all, despite its macabre events, and probably served to encourage her not to be afraid to open up painful areas in her life.

In the following dream a young professional woman (the dreamer) is given a picture of a "sickness unto death":

> There is an insensitive man who has custody of a young girl of six or seven. I am living in a big old house and each time I see the girl, she is looking progressively worse until finally she is crawling down a dirt road, dying from lack of nourishment. I am concerned about her, but I don't know how to get her away from the man (her father), particularly since I have no idea where he is during the periods when he disappears.

Some part of her (perhaps only six or seven years old) is "dying from lack of nourishment." Whatever that part of her is, is caught in the father. Like a complex that is only constellated at times, the father "disappears" for periods, so she doesn't know how to get the girl away from him. The "father" may refer either to her personal father's set of attitudes which she still holds to her detriment or it may refer to a generalized authority problem. The power of the image of this pitiful child may help the dreamer explore the parts of herself that lack nourishment.

A young wife and mother, trying to discover her identity and vocation over and beyond those roles dreamed:

> Our family was swimming. My daughter could swim a little, but I told her she had to stay in the shallow end. My husband and I were sitting by the pool, talking to relatives, and I saw my daughter standing by the deep end. I yelled at her, but she didn't hear me, and jumped in. I started taking off my shoes and jeans and telling my husband she was going to drown. He didn't seem to be paying much attention. I ran over to the pool, and I couldn't see her on the bottom. I dove in and couldn't find her. I asked the lifeguard who was on a stand if she could see her on the bottom. She said, "Yes." I asked her to help me to get her. She said she couldn't, but would go find help. I dove back in and got her. When I brought her up, she was unconscious. I was hysterical and thought she was dead. I wasn't even aware of what was going on around me. Finally, my husband got through to me that she was O.K. The male

lifeguard had resuscitated her. Then I got furious at the lifeguard who had refused to help. I said I was going to sue the pool.

Some part of the dreamer is about to "drown" in the unconscious. The dreamer is fearful about that part of herself (represented by the daughter) getting into deep water (dream work?), but it happens. She can't find the girl at first, and the female lifeguard (a shadow figure of her own femininity?) refuses to dive in although she sees the girl on the bottom of the pool. The dreamer accomplishes the rescue, and the girl is brought back to life by the male lifeguard, but the dreamer does not know it until her husband "finally got through" to her that the girl was all right.

The dream gives a picture of her life situation and points to the necessity for some animus development and awareness in the dreamer in order to prevent the death of some potential in her. About three weeks later the same dreamer had another dream about a lost, possibly dead, child:

> I dreamed I was sitting in church, and they announced that two couples who are our closest friends had had their children lost and kidnapped the day before. I was shocked and very upset. I ran to the back to talk to them. One couple thought they would get their child back that day. The other couple didn't know where their baby was. The mother was hysterical. I was hugging her and crying, too. Somebody walked up and said her baby was dead, and she started screaming. I was holding her and in a little while her husband walked up and said the baby had been found and was fine. We were all so happy.

This time one could say that the as-yet-undeveloped part of herself feels not so much drowned in the unconscious as stolen from her— "kidnapped." The doubling effect (two shadow couples with stolen children) suggests that the issue in the dreamer's life may be closer to consciousness and one about which she feels conflict. Again it is the husband (a positive animus figure for the dreamer) who reassures her that the baby has "been found and was fine."

Shadow figures in dreams are not, as we have said, necessarily negative. They may portray other aspects of the psyche, potentialities or new possibilities, which, once recognized, would be welcomed as a part of life. Wallace had a series of "death" dreams in which he (1) shook hands with a dead man, (2) was planning to kill a friend, (3) learned that his life was to be "spared," and (4) had killed someone and might kill another. Without an appreciation of the symbolic language of dreams and the subjective approach to dream interpretation, that series could be rather frightening. As it is, we have come to see it as a series of dreams involving Wallace's relation to his vocation. Though they were only partly understood at the time, they do reveal the strivings in the unconscious as he moved along his life's journey, and we feel they were an influence on the conscious decisions he made.

The first dream in the series came in the spring of 1964. At this time, Wallace had been a parish priest in the Episcopal Church for nearly four years, serving two "mission" churches. They were eight miles apart, and he drove back and forth between them several times on Sunday and most other days of the week as well. It kept him very busy. He liked what he was doing and poured himself into his work. Earlier in life he had experienced a "leading from God" that he must "go to seminary" and had just assumed that meant being a parish priest. He was very happy in his vocational choice, though he sometimes worried about neglecting the family and not spending enough time with the children. Wallace had loved his study while in seminary and as those three years had drawn to a close had, on one occasion, said to Jean that he wished he could teach in seminary. The desire had not been considered further, however, as there was no money for the further education which would be required. On leaving seminary, he had subscribed to the scholarly journals which he had enjoyed, but they stacked up on his bookshelf, for he never had time to read them. Here is the dream:

> I dreamed that President Kennedy, who had been shot, was in a casket that was open and people were filing by to look at him. It was in the rotunda of the nation's capitol building. I moved along in the line and when I got to the casket, he was propped up on some pillows; I reached out my hand to shake hands with him. When I took his hand it felt warm, and I said to him, "There is a lot of life yet in you; it is a shame for you to be buried; your father has a lot of money; you should go away, perhaps to some island; you can still read and write; just let them bury the casket."

Wallace had first heard about Jung's psychology in November, 1962, and had done a little reading during his summer vacation in 1963, but he had no idea what that dream could be about. A friend of ours who gave lectures on Jung's psychology suggested that President Kennedy was a part of Wallace and that he must feel like he was being buried. It was news to Wallace that he felt like he was half-dead and about to be buried. Later in the week our friend telephoned Jean, as she had remembered that Wallace's father had died the previous November (actually the same week that President Kennedy was shot), and she thought perhaps the reference in the dream to "father's money" might be to an inheritance. Jean told her there had been none, but that perhaps in Wallace's case it might be the "heavenly" father, and our friend agreed.

Life went on as usual, but about a month later, without planning, seeking, or searching on our part, we were both offered a joint grant for study at the C. G. Jung Institute in Zurich, Switzerland. Reflection on Wallace's dream probably prepared us both, without our realizing it at the time, for making the decision to accept the grant.

At the time of making the decision for study, Wallace did not plan to leave the parish ministry, but simply took that opportunity to learn more about the psyche and the spiritual world. However, the unconscious was "seeing ahead," as perhaps the following dream suggests. Wallace did not understand this dream fragment at the time and had found it rather puzzling, almost disturbing. The dream occurred two days after his last Sunday as pastor of the two churches. Here is the sketchy fragment that was recorded:

> I dreamed I was—for some reason I didn't know—plotting the murder of my friend Don. The dream kept worrying with how to do it and not get caught . . . maybe if I got him to sleep, but how to do that? . . . and what about a postmortem? . . . many plans, never executed.

Don was pastor of the nearest church. He and Wallace were friends. They had often discussed the similarity of their approaches, their liturgy, and even their vestments—which suggests a similar persona as parish priests. The dream suggests that the vocational question is not resolved but has been called into question. The unconscious often seems to use hyperbole as if to get our attention—for example, a *murder* of the parish priest.

Near the end of the first year of study in Zurich, Wallace had the following dream:

> I was a young man and we lived in a society with a primitive

organization, that is, very strong tribal feelings, etc. I had been schooled and educated more than the other young men in my village which was on the edge of the sea. A great war was approaching. Someway there were to be some who fought or did something that meant they would probably not live; and there was a way for some to survive in all likelihood. I knew I was to survive, that it was "right"—in the dream I thought: I "know" this the way turtles know what is destined. It was not "wrong" for me to choose to save myself. My father would find it difficult to choose his son to be spared, as he was head of the village and had to set an example for them. I decided to ask my grandfather about it. But the one who appeared was my great-grandfather (not anyone I ever knew). He said "yes"—I should come with him. I expressed the thought that I disliked leaving my father, but my mother said he would be glad to be relieved of the responsibility of the decision and would be glad for me. There would be no question of disapproval in the village, as great-grandfather's authority in the family surpassed all other. I awoke with a feeling that the matter was resolved.

There is a lot going on in that dream—correlations with Wallace's personal and family history—which we will not elaborate upon here. However, it can be said that Wallace's family is rather "tribal" in its organization, with strong family feelings and a sense of responsibility to the family. There are clergy ancestors on both sides, and it was a very "acceptable" thing to the family when he became a parish clergyman. In the dream, his father probably represents the kind of outer social pressure for conformity, as he had held respected positions in the community. On the local level, in the hometown of Wallace's childhood, it might have been considered embarrassing to "leave one's post" in the parish ministry. Great-grandfather is an archetypal figure, representing something transcendent. His authority surpasses all others, the dream says, and he says "yes"—it is right that Wallace's life be spared. And Wallace awoke with the feeling that the matter was resolved.

The dream did not say what "matter was resolved," and at the time Wallace did not see this dream in vocational terms. But deep down, some "matter was resolved." The dream puts it rather strongly for him: his life is to be "spared."

Near the middle of our second year in Zurich, Wallace had written his bishop inquiring about a parish appointment. Then Wallace had this dream:

I dreamed that I had killed someone in Israel and that I was going back to Israel to settle it—it would be "paid for" there. The killing seemed impersonal as I did not remember anything about the person killed. I was sorry that I had, that was all. It seemed that someone would have to die when I went back, though the killing of someone else did not seem to be the way . . . (the dream ended unresolved).

This dream presents the matter clearly. "Someone in Israel" is obviously the parish priest in Wallace; to go back to another parish assignment is pictured as "paying for the crime" of having left the parish (or killing the parish priest). The dream points out that this action means the death of someone else. It now seems clear that going back would mean the death of the student-who-wants-to-be-a-teacher part of Wallace. Actually, subsequent events led eventually to his being offered a further grant to get a Ph.D. at the University of Chicago. That, of course, made possible the teaching career in religion and psychology which has followed ever since.

This dream series is an example of how dreams do present aspects of one's life and, if brought to consciousness, clarify the nature of the choices being presented. Further, it seems to us that this dream series indicates that even though one may not understand them clearly, just by paying enough attention to write dreams down—doing that much "listening"—one may be aided in making the needed conscious choices.

Finally, some death dreams are best understood not so much (or not only) on the subjective level, but rather on the objective level. We like to think of these as "gift" dreams. In his posthumously published *Memories, Dreams, Reflections,* Jung tells of a dream he had of his wife after her death in which she appeared before him. He thought of it as a "portrait" she had commissioned for him. She appeared in her prime, yet the portrait contained the whole of their relationship and gave Jung a powerful sense that she was free.

While Wallace was serving a parish, one of his parishioners had what we call a "gift" dream—a gift from God. The dreamer's husband had a heart attack and was seriously ill for some two or three weeks. On one occasion when Wallace was visiting the husband in the hospital, he encountered the wife running down the hall hysterically crying and rather out of control—she had misunderstood something a nurse said and thought her husband was dead. Wallace discovered the facts and helped her regain composure. A few days later, perhaps a week, Wallace received a call in the middle of the night to come to her house and tell the children about their father's death. The wife and mother was calm and at peace when she met him, much to Wallace's surprise. Later, she told him of the dream which had come to her that night just before the hospital called to tell her of her husband's death. She dreamed that she was sitting by her husband's hospital bed (which she had been doing so much during the illness) when Jesus came into the room to the other side of the bed. He looked across the bed directly at her with a loving, tender look; then he picked up her husband and carried him out of the room. She said that when she awoke she knew her husband was dead and that it was all right. It was no surprise when the hospital called. Her grief was no less, but she had an inner peace about her husband that nothing took from her—a priceless gift.

It has been our experience that such objective dreams of death have uniformly served such a purpose of bringing new strength and peace to the dreamer.

• 15

Other Transformation Motifs

The patterns and images of growth and transformation are so many and varied that they could never all be listed. The human psyche is a deep imaginative well from which the images come to each dreamer with precision. In this chapter we will first direct attention to the general theory of psychological types and its relevance to transformation. Then we will explore dreams about a variety of motifs of transformation. The selection of motifs, since it could never be exhaustive, will at least, we hope, be suggestive and evocative. In each transformation image, a fundamental change of attitude is suggested to the dreamer.

Jung's insights into people's differing psychological types can be an aid to discovering the directions in which their growth needs to go. He discovered that people are basically different in some ways which can be helpfully categorized. He suggests that people have two basic attitudinal types, which he named extravert and introvert. Though these terms have entered ordinary conversation, Jung's definitions are different from the way the terms are customarily used.

Jung says the difference has to do with energy flow. The extravert's energy flow is outward, to other people, to ideas or objects. The extravert's energy flows outward and makes a relationship with the person, idea, or object out there. The introvert's energy flow goes outward, but then the person, idea, or object is, in effect, brought back into the introvert. The relationship is made inside. Then, as Wallace, who is an introvert, likes to say, "The introvert may or may not come back out and let you know what the relationship is."

The United States is a culture with a strong extraverted tendency; many people who might actually prefer the introverted attitude may have adapted to the prevailing extraversion. The reverse is probably true in some countries of northern Europe like Switzerland and England. The U.S. adaptation is so strong that many American-based psychological theories tend to sound as if introversion is not an acceptable way of being; they view introversion as a pathology of which one needs to be cured. This probably accounts in part for the popularity of Jungian psychology among introverts; Jung, himself an introvert, understood the phenomenon as healthy and acceptable.

Though these two attitudes are at opposite ends of a spectrum, Jung says all of us actually do both. In fact, the goal of wholeness is to be able to move between the two poles in a rhythm which is comfortable. All extraverts need to move into their inner space some of the time, and all introverts need to let their energy flow outward. Most people, though, have a preference for one way or the other, one way of being which suits them better. Sometimes it is hard to determine what this preference is because one has been taught the opposite way of being, even without conscious intention on the part of the teachers. If the parents of a family are both of one attitudinal preference, the children may have been unconsciously programmed that the parent's way is the right way. One can be so taught either by following the pattern of someone admired or by rebelling against the pattern of someone who is disliked. However, most people find that they can tell what their preference is after some reflection.

There are two reasons it is helpful to decide whether your preference is for extraversion or introversion. The first is the comfort level that is experienced by settling into the preferred type—which has been compared to settling your feet into old, familiar house shoes. From this relaxed acceptance of the attitudinal preference, people seem able to function more efficiently, with less loss of energy and less strain. The other reason is becoming aware of the direction of needed growth— in the development of the other side. Extraverts who see introversion as a way of growth for themselves find introversion an interesting new dwelling with many fascinating rooms to explore—as long as they don't have to live there all the time. Introverts find that a bit of unforced extraversion can be not only fulfilling, but even fun, once they know they don't have to take up permanent residence.

What has happened to all too many people, whichever the primary attitude is, has been a sense of uncertainty about themselves and about how others view them. The process of projection works here as well as in other areas, and most people, without being aware that they are doing so, interpret other people's actions as if the others were thinking what they themselves would be thinking if they behaved as the others do.

We have realized that much of our interaction early in our marriage operated out of just such misapprehension of each other. In such a typical event, Jean would have an idea that she thought would be fun for a given evening, and she would begin to tell Wallace about it as soon as they left the carpool and arrived home. At the end of her excited (extraverted) suggestion of the idea, she would expect Wallace to react with some measure of enthusiasm at once. Wallace, unlocking the door, anxious to get his tie off, focused elsewhere, would reply with some sort of noncommittal (introverted) sound.

Jung says the introvert has an automatic "no" to any suggestion, and Wallace thinks this is because they are buying time while they process the suggestions inwardly—which sometimes takes longer than the outward processing of the extravert. Certainly it takes longer than the impatience of the expectant extravert wants it to, especially if the extravert is unaware of these basic attitudinal differences.

In this typical exchange between the Clifts, Jean would feel quite crushed at Wallace's lack of response. She would assume that he was thinking what she would be thinking if she had responded in such lukewarm fashion, and so she would think, "He hates the idea!" Then she would have to go off to the bedroom and try to forgive him, not only for not liking the idea, but even more for being too "chicken" to speak up and say so. So now he was in trouble not only for not liking the idea (her assumption, though she did not know this) but for not speaking up bravely to disagree with her. She, on the other hand, felt quite "holy" for being so forgiving.

As this innocent couple moved inevitably to the showdown neither expected, Wallace had meanwhile processed Jean's idea and decided that her plan did sound like it might be fun, so he sauntered into the kitchen where she was cheerfully humming a happy tune (he says, looking back on it, that he might with sensitivity have detected a forced quality to her gaiety) and told her that he would like to spend the evening as she had suggested. Then came her explosion. (The hidden thought she had was, "Brother, it's too late! I've forgiven you!") So Jean was exploding, and Wallace was thinking, self-righteously, "Now what have I done? All I did was say I liked her idea. It doesn't even help when you agree with her!" The awful thing about such exchanges (other than how common they are between extraverts and introverts) is that both people feel justified and misunderstood and mistreated.

After a number of such interactions, both at home and in the world, people may not only decide that the family and the people at work are impossible, but they probably begin to suspect that there are basic personality problems with themselves. Extraverts get afraid that they talk too much, are too dominant, and that people will never like them. Introverts get afraid that they are too slow, are pushovers for other people, and that people will never like them.

Quite small children exhibit the typical patterns of one type or the other; many mothers feel that they can tell in the hospital which type their newborn babies prefer. We noticed that Wallace could feed our son his baby food in the high-chair stage better than Jean, and when we analyzed what he did that was different, we saw that Jean, in "offering" the food, tended to push it directly toward our introverted son. Wallace, without having realized he was doing so, offered the food, was not surprised when the baby turned his head, and consequently took the baby's wordless "automatic no" as a "wait a minute," and had the food available when the baby was ready. This has continued to be a good clue for us of how it feels to an introvert to have all that energy coming directly at him. The same son, when he was older, gave us another good clue. When his mother was trying to get him to make a decision one time, he said, "Mom, I think I could decide if you just wouldn't look at me." Many introverts resonate with this preference to escape the palpable energy flow of extravert attention.

Extraverts sometimes experience introverts as looking bored or looking as if they have stopped processing a decision. The extravert may consequently push for a decision, fearing the loss of attention. The introvert may actually have just begun to process the decision. If the extravert will leave the introvert alone for a bit, the decision can be dealt with more creatively.

Jung also identified four different modes of functioning, which can be diagramed on a circle, with two pairs of opposites. The opposite ways of perceiving or taking in data are called sensation and intuition. The sensate person takes in data through the five senses of seeing, hearing, smelling, tasting, and touching. Sensate people are thus well oriented to the outer world and to the here and now. The intuitive perceiver takes in data, Jung says, through the unconscious. The intuitive is likely to say, "I don't know how I know what I know. I just know." This sounds absurd to a non-intuitive, who is likely to dismiss the intuitions. Intuitives are not well oriented to the here and now but tend to focus on implications and possibilities in the future. They make leaps which they cannot explain, but which remarkably often turn out to be accurate. As with extraversion and introversion, everyone tends to have a preferred way of perceiving and to be correspondingly weak in the opposite mode.

The opposite ways of judging, deciding, or evaluating are two rational functions which Jung called thinking and feeling. The thinking function evaluates objectively on the basis of logic; the feeling function evaluates subjectively on the basis of value and human relationship. The thinking function names and classifies in an abstract manner. The feeling function evaluates and relates to the human factors in a situation. As with the other opposites, everyone tends to prefer one mode and to be weak in the opposite.

Though each person has one perferred mode in each of these pairs of opposite ways of functioning, each one also has one of the four which is *dominant*. The function opposite to the dominant function is referred to as the fourth function or the *inferior* function. As part of the movement toward growth and wholeness, each individual needs to become more skilled in each of the ways of functioning. Everyone does all of the four, of course, as there are some activities which require each different function, but some are much easier to develop than others. Jung says that no matter how much one develops the functions, one of them, the inferior function, will always be partly in the unconscious and so will be very difficult. One will tend to be awkward with it, make gaffes and mistakes with it, remain somewhat primitive in its use. In fact, the inability to function well with the inferior function may well be the clearest clue to determining which function is dominant.

In recent years, increasing use has been made of questionnaires which seek to help determine what one's preferences are between these pairs of opposites. "The Jungian Type Survey: The Gray-Wheelwrights Test" was developed by Jungian analysts, and the "Myers Briggs Type Indicator" (MBTI) was developed by two American women, a mother and daughter. Both tools can be useful in determining where one's preferences fall, though in some cases (especially when one has become adapted to another mode) it is difficult to be certain.

As indicated, Jung's theory of psychological types is not only oriented to understanding oneself and other people but is also focused on developing the other sides of oneself, to being more whole persons. It is here that an understanding of types may help in interpreting dreams. When you begin to associate and amplify a dream figure, whether shadow, anima, or animus, one of the associations may well be a dominant attitude or function of the dream figure. You are then able to understand the dream as making some comment on your own psychological type and its use and development.

Sometimes the dreams themselves refer to type directly. Wallace had a humorous dream shortly after he became familiar with Jung's typology:

> There was a collection of shell-like sea things. Some moved; each had a different movement, just as chess pieces do, but these were self-moving. K. took out one of four objects, and it jumped around and pecked at things. She said it was the thinking function. Then she took out another one from the back, which was furry, like a child's toy. She said it doesn't "kneel," but it did move around.

Wallace himself is a thinking type, and our friend K. is a feeling type. Her characterization of thinking type (her inferior function) as jumping around and pecking at things struck Wallace as humorously accurate, though a bit derogatory, as people are inclined to be about their inferior function. The feeling function (his inferior function) came "from the back," and his view of it was that it was like a child's toy—one's inferior function usually is out of sight, at the back, and likely to be childish and viewed as childish. Yet the caution at the end of the dream is an important caution for everyone in connection with the inferior function: it does not kneel—one cannot control or command it, or ever bring it completely within consciousness. It is this very unavailability of the inferior function which, on the negative side, makes people so touchy about it. One is inclined to be irritated with people who suggest that one is not good at what one is not good at. On the positive side, it has been suggested that some of the most transcendent experiences of life also come through the inferior function—again, probably because one cannot control that area, so there is room for God to come through it.

As we said, there is an endless variety of other symbols of transformation, some of which we will explore in the remainder of this chapter. Not only hero journeys, but any journey motif suggests the possibility of change, particularly one which moves from one kind of place to another. The specific details of each dream can be studied for clues to the direction and issues surrounding the change. Such dreams can be very simple, like this one:

> I am walking across a bridge over a street. It connects a new and an old building. It seems temporary, like it could be drawn back. A lot of flowers are there.

The dreamer is making a movement in her life which connects the old and new, but there is a tenuous quality in the bridge, which can be drawn back. The dreamer's situation is clear in this psychic snapshot; she may draw back. There is encouragement for her to go on, though, in the flowers. This is usually a positive symbol, but is especially so in her case because she is a thinking type, and flowers are associated with feelings. Flowers are given on joyful and sad occasions; they speak of love and caring.

We have several times referred to kitchens as places where transformation takes place. In kitchens people take food and make it available for nourishment. This dreamer's kitchen dream seemed to urge her to "get on with it":

> The setting is an island, very small. I am in the kitchen. Every signal goes off simultaneously. The toast pops up, the timer on the stove buzzes, the water for the coffee starts to boil, the alarm clock is ringing in the bedroom. I stand there and cannot decide what to take care of first.

It is easy to sense the dreamer's confusion and feeling of being stuck and alone (the small island). Yet the dream, with its homely imagery, gives a comfortable sense that, confused as she may feel, the problems really can be dealt with. She just needs to decide where to begin and then—begin.

In addition to cooking, other chemical processes also transform. Jung came to understand alchemy with all its processes and intricacies as a rich and complex symbol of the psychic transformation process. Jung and his followers have followed the clues from these esoteric writings as a source of understanding different phases of the human individuation process.

Dreams of waking up from sleep can signify coming to a new awareness or consciousness, or warnings to wake up can be cautions not to "sleep" through life and its possibilities. Once, the night before she was to visit an author about whom she had heard a great deal, Jean dreamed that she did not get up when the alarm went off and slept through her appointment time. The dream was warning that Jean needed to be very awake, so as not to miss out on the experience of truly encountering the wise lady with whom she had an appointment.

Similarly, another dreamer, just terminating some counseling, dreamed that she was talking on the telephone to her counselor in a pleasant conversation. As they were hanging up, her counselor said, "Goodby, and wake up, honey." She felt it was a warning not to stop her continuing dialogue with the unconscious just because she was not directly engaged in regular counseling.

Nightmares and other threatening dreams sometimes end with the thought: "I have to wake up and stop this from happening." This seems to be not only a lucid dream in which the dreamer realizes it is a dream and wants out of it, but even more deeply, a suggestion that increased awareness of the dreamer's personal involvement in the threatening situation can avoid the catastrophe.

One man reported a series of dreams over a period of twelve years with the continuing theme that he was in the death house awaiting execution. Then the pattern changed dramatically one night:

> I am in death row ready to be executed in the electric chair. Suddenly the doors of the prison open wide, and I find myself free, walking out the gates.

He saw that although he was a creative person, he had a pattern of joining groups that were oppressive and authoritarian—murdering his own freedom. The dream coincided with a decision he made to leave an authoritarian institution behind and become the genuine human being he could be, with his own internal symbols leading him to freedom.

One person who felt somewhat fearful of what might happen if she opened herself to the unconscious through dream work was reassured by this dream:

> There was a huge pool full of blue water. As a demonstration one of the two kids threw a bomb into the water. It did not damage the pool—just made the blue water clear. Then the bomb fell through a trap door to a pool below, doing the same thing, then again through to another pool doing the same thing again.

Even though she encounters a "bomb" in her dream work, the dream imagery suggests that there will be no damage done—only a clearing of the pools of water, no matter how deep the bomb goes.

The loss of teeth is a common and somewhat puzzling symbol of change. Freud said one could never fully interpret teeth dreams. Because of the order in which they appear, teeth can represent the increasing growth of a person. The loss of baby teeth and the slow appearance of "permanent" teeth is part of the pattern of maturing, and the loss of teeth in old age can be seen as a part of the loss of power. People speak of "biting off more than they can chew" and not being able "to get my teeth into" a difficult problem. Knocking out front teeth is quite an old part of some initiation rites. "Chewing on" an issue may help in the analysis of the important factors, so that they can be assimilated into consciousness, just as chewing on food with the teeth enables its assimilation into the body. All in all, teeth dreams are associated with some transition times and the possibility either of regression to babyhood, anxiety over aging or the loss of power, or of really "getting the teeth into" some possibility.

One woman in mid-life had two successive loss-of-teeth dreams while trying to decide on her future direction. She was between jobs and having difficulty discerning what she wanted to do next. The first dream contained clues to its interpretation:

> I was cleaning the bathroom. My gums were sore and bleeding, and when I looked in the mirror, I saw I had lost the two teeth from the upper front left side.
> Then my glasses fell apart. I felt this was symbolic, so I prayed that God would help me see what I wasn't seeing.

The dreamer associated losing her "eye" tooth with breaking her glasses and took the hint from the last part of the dream that she was missing something in her attempt to discern her future goals. Three weeks later the motif was repeated:

> My teeth were loose. The right eye tooth fell out and the left eye tooth was about to. Someone said I should check with the dentist for some medicine for my gums, which were wearing away and not holding the teeth. As I dressed to go to the dentist upstairs, a friend called one and got a prescription. I wasn't sure I should take it without a dentist seeing me first.

The second dream confirmed for the dreamer her interpretation of the first dream and added the further warning that she must look carefully for the specific "medicine" for herself, even though helpful and well-meaning friends offered their aid.

Teeth dreams seem to come at difficult times in the dreamers' lives, and they frequently seem to advise getting some help—whether from God or the dentist. One troubled woman dreamed:

> I dreamed my husband and I were riding in a car in the mountains. I bit down on something hard like a nut. I couldn't chew it, so I started to pull pieces out of my mouth. Then I realized my mouth really hurt and some of my teeth were loose. I started spitting out teeth. My mouth was swollen and very painful. We stopped at a store, and I looked in the phone book for dentists. I asked the girl behind the desk for the name of a good dentist. She said there was one upstairs. When I got upstairs, the office was under construction and was very dirty and messy. There was also a long line of people waiting to talk to the receptionist.

She had known there were a lot of problems besetting her, but this dream highlighted that her outer life was too "hard a nut to crack" or chew. She saw this as a strong emblem of the painful time she was in the midst of, and she knew she needed help, even though there might be some dirty and messy aspects to be dealt with. As with the previous dreamer she needed to go "upstairs" for help.

The specific need for counseling was mentioned to another dreamer:

> I am distressed because three of my front teeth have fallen out—the left eye tooth and the ones on either side of it. I don't know why they have fallen out. I am scared and mortified, so I go to my psychiatrist for help.

The dreamer had never been to a psychiatrist, but the dream helped her decide that she did need some professional help in some life situations she could no longer ignore.

We have also mentioned previously the remodeling of a house or finding a new wing of a house as images of change and growth. Helpers are frequently encountered in these tasks, and rather specific directions suggested. Wallace dreamed once that he found a new wing of his house which he did not know was there. Among other things it held a grand piano. The dream probably had many meanings, but on a very practical one, it inspired him to begin playing music again—something which he had formerly loved to do, but had neglected in the busyness of his life—a refound joy for him.

The healing or changing in dreams sometimes has a very religious quality, indicating its importance to us. One woman dreamed:

> I was in a church or chapel. People were going up to the priest, like for communion, but instead he was anointing each with the sign of the cross on their foreheads. I hesitated, but then decided to go up after all. I was the last one in the left line. When I got to the priest, he asked me to anoint him.

Not only is the significance of the dream indicated by the religious symbols, but there is also the powerful sense of mutual blessing inherent in the indication that the dreamer herself has the power of her own healing within herself.

Specific healing motifs sometimes appear in dreams, not only describing the fact of healing, but carrying such numinous power for the dreamer that they seem to accomplish it:

> It is summertime and I am in the kitchen of a big, old frame house. A middle-aged Chicano woman is in the kitchen with me and we are talking about my grandmother and her failing capacities. I tell her about Alzheimer's disease and the confusion she is experiencing. The woman says she can heal this infirmity. She goes over and gets a compress of steaming herbs and places one portion below my navel. She then raises her arms and moves them across my body, blessing me, chanting in a strange tongue as she does so. I look at her and the room begins to vibrate from the force of her power. I am shaken by the experience and stand there wondering how to continue when my friend J. comes in dressed in a long skirt and I tell her the woman is healing with the teas. She says, yes, that is how it is done and I say that the strange thing is that she is healing my grandmother by applying the herbs to me. I awoke and could feel the force of the dream.

This dreamer was close to her grandmother, who in fact did have such failing powers. However, the dream hints that there may be subjective significance for the dreamer, because the healing acts are performed on her. She felt the need for healing, particularly in one close relationship, about which she felt depression and despair. Two months before this dream, reflecting on her depressed state, she wrote in her journal: "Although sad, I don't cry, and though tired, I can't sleep. I'm rarely hungry and I have a vision of my grandmother sitting in her armchair in her old Victorian house, hands in her lap, twiddling her thumbs, staring off into a place which I cannot see . . . ." It is this despairing person within her which the healer addresses.

She had a high respect for the wisdom of the Chicano healer, and the dream stayed present to her. In what seemed coincidental to her, this long-time, deep-seated breach in the relationship began to be healed during the week that followed the dream.

Jung discussed many times the importance of the royal marriage in dreams as a coming together of the opposites deep within the dreamer. Jungian analyst and author James Hall has suggested that any wedding mentioned even casually in dreams is a signal that a transformation is possible through this kind of union of opposites.

One young mother dreamed such a wedding dream, typical of those which signal that a union of apparent opposites in our lives is possible:

> I dreamed that I was in a dormitory room, and my husband and I were supposed to get ready to go to a wedding. There were all these clothes hanging on racks. I was looking for one particular dress to wear, but neither of us could find it. I didn't recognize any of the clothes and asked him where they all came from. He said some strange woman brought them for me. I didn't like them; they were the wrong size. I was frustrated, finally put on something, but didn't like the way I looked.

This motif not only signals the possible reconciling union of the wedding but seems to carry the same kind of warning motif in the biblical parable of the wedding guests without the proper clothes. The dream seems to encourage her to be very careful to find her own "clothes" in whatever direction she decides to go.

A powerful wedding dream came to a professional woman who had been exploring various possibilities of meaning and religion in her life. Despite her success at work, she also wanted to be in touch with her own deep feminine nature. She dreamed:

> I am at my wedding in a Catholic church. I am dressed in a long homespun handmade linen dress. I am in the second row from the altar and the priest or priestess is giving out fresh fruit in the form of communion, much as one would make offerings to the Buddha. The row in front of me and across the aisle is filled with women of many cultures, each dressed in the costume of her country. I particularly remember vividly the Polynesian and African women. Each woman goes forward to receive the offering; but when it is

> my turn, I feel very self-conscious and unable to make myself approach the altar, although I would like to, or at least I believe that I should. The woman next to me is a dark-haired young woman whom I believe to be the Virgin Mary. She senses my reluctance and begins talking softly to me. I talk with her for a while and then realize that she is speaking to me in Spanish. Although my Spanish is very limited, I can understand what she is saying.

The dreamer's associations with all the symbols in the dream were very positive—the Catholic church, Buddhism, the various nationalities of women and the Spanish language. This dream is a powerful gathering of positive feminine symbols: Mother church, the homespun handmade dress, the fresh fruit, as well as all the gathered women, even to the Virgin Mary. As she works to be in touch with her deep nature, she certainly has a lot of help to call on.

A sense of the process of change around a specific issue, such as one's femininity, can be seen in this series of three dreams of a religious sister in mid-life. She had reached the point where she felt she needed to reexamine her attitudes about sexuality. She had grown up with some negative attitudes and a false sense of guilt. This had stunted her growth toward sexual maturity. Much that was within her had been pushed down. She came to realize that a greater interior freedom was needed and that this would enable her to live more fully her femininity and to relate more effectively with people around her without meaning that she needed to desert her chosen celibate life style. When she began to work with her dreams, the following dream was experienced when she was taking a workshop on sexuality.

> I guide into a church a young woman who is blind. I try to find a seat for her, but all the seats are wobbly and old—so too is the floor of this dilapidated church building. I find a chair for her, but there is a step just behind it, and I fear she may move slightly and fall, but there doesn't seem to be any safer place in the church. She's very dependent on my putting her in the best, safest, most satisfactory place in the church.

The imagery in the dream showed the sister just where she was in relation to her shadow, which she saw as a femininity which was blind and had been in a dilapidated set of attitudes. The dream gave her the courage to realize she needed to be on the journey to find a better "place to sit in the church."

Two years later, the same sister had the following dream, which again coincided with a seminar on sexual morality:

> A child and I were sitting looking out a window of something like a guest house when I saw a koala in a tree outside. I felt really excited. I drew the boy's attention to it. It looked like a big gray tabby cat without a tail. It then seemed to walk out on a limb, which I could not see. It looked like he was walking up into fresh air, but I presumed it must have a fine limb that we couldn't see.

After this dream, the sister used her journal and wrote a dialogue with the koala, which she experienced as a delightful exchange. The little animal, warm, soft, cuddly, yet with claws, symbolized for her the affective area of her life. The koala, so sleepy in the daytime, represented her femininity which had been, as it were, put to sleep over many years. As the two "dialogued" about the invisible tree limb, the sister realized that the seminar had surfaced within her some fears that she was "out on a limb" with her newfound sense of freedom in her attitudes. The dream clarified for her the new stance; she just did not want to return to her old attitudes of fear and guilt. She wanted to develop to full potential the warmth and love that was deep within her. The transience of a guest house would seem to indicate that this fear of "being out on a limb" was not a permanent thing.

Six months later she dreamed:

> I was in a big college and while everyone was quietly engaged in work, the superior was outside having fun. He was waltzing around with a koala in his arms. In fact, he tried to get a big matronly lady to dance with him, but she was bashful, so he then took the koala in his arms.

The sister, who had always had a great sense of responsibility and had held positions of leadership within her congregation, saw in the dream that the "superior" in her needed to play, to dance—that there needed to be a happier and closer relationship between her masculine leadership qualities and her own feminine warmth. The dream was very positive. It pointed to a coming together of these two aspects of herself in a delightful image of dancing with a koala.

In all their incredible complexity, the dreams continue, night after night, around the globe and throughout time, to produce kaleidoscopes of imagery, each tailor-made for the dreamer on that particular night. Of them all, none is more numinous and mysterious than those discussed in the next chapter.

•16

The Self

Perhaps Jung's most important insights concern the archetype of wholeness, the archetype of the Self. By the term *Self,* Jung did not refer to the more ordinary usage of the conscious personality; for the center of consciousness, he used the term *ego.* In some ways, his choice of the word *Self* is unfortunate because it is subject to that misapprehension. In Jung's terminology, the Self is the ordering and unifying center of the total psyche (conscious and unconscious), while at the same time the Self is the whole sphere—the Self is both center and circumference of the psyche. The Self thus incorporates all the other archetypes into a paradoxical unity, transcending any attempt to contain or define it.

Jung saw this central archetype as the organizer and inventor of the dream images—the inner guiding factor that continually extends and matures the personality when the ego is willing to listen to the messages of the Self. The ego perceives the Self as "other," and the subjective experience conveys the feeling that "some suprapersonal force is actively interfering in a creative way. One sometimes feels that the unconscious is leading the way in accordance with a secret design."[1] The Self is the instigator and director of the process of individuation. Jung spoke of the Self as the "god image" in the psyche, and encounters with the Self have all the qualities associated with the concept of God.

Speaking as a psychologist, Jung said the idea of the Self was a construct necessary to account for such experiences of the psyche. He did not offer the Self as any kind of "proof" of the existence of God, but he observed the universal need for a sense of meaning in life and the human experience of a response to that need. Thus, with those for whom a traditional religious symbol system still functions (as it does for us), Jung's concept of the Self accords with their religious experience in which the transcendent has become immanent.

The process of individuation itself—the movement toward a conscious process of becoming human and whole—usually begins with some wounding or shock or inability to function. Then images or experiences of the Self appear as a support for one who no longer feels able to be at one or to be unified. A sense of dividedness or separation seems to have been basic to the human condition, probably since the coming to consciousness, and the vocational "call" to wholeness arises in moments of special conflict or crisis. Every human heart longs for the overcoming of that sense of alienation. As we discussed in the chapter on symbolism, some sense of being connected to a larger reality is basic to healing that separation and finding meaning in life.

The Jungian analyst Edward Edinger has called the Self the "organ of acceptance." The experience of the Self, for the ego, is an experience of acceptance and of being "at one." In psychotherapy, the Self is often projected upon the therapist, and it is the acceptance of the therapist which makes possible the healing. The Self is also frequently projected on the professional religious figure, where acceptance of the "sinner" creates the same healing experience. Acceptance in all the depths of its meaning is, of course, what true love is all about. In one sense or another, the traditions of the world's religions and many of the world's philosophies have been directed toward this acceptance, focus, and resolution of apparently irreconcilable conflicts which the power and authority of the encounters with the Self carry.

Jung says that those who have developed a kind of dialogue between the ego and the rest of the psyche sense themselves as the objects of an unknown and supraordinate subject. He closed his *Answer to Job* with this passage:

> Even the enlightened person remains what he is, and is never more than his own limited ego before the One who dwells within him, whose form has no knowable boundaries, who encompasses him on all sides, fathomless as the abysms of the earth and vast as the sky.[2]

These descriptions are remarkably like those of many Christian writers. Jung quotes, for example, the seventeenth-century German hymnist Angelus Silesius, "God is my centre when I close him in, and my circumference when I melt in him."[3] Thomas Merton's biographer describes him as one of the few in the twentieth century who followed in the footsteps of the saints in love and self-forgetfulness "as if they had found a center outside the ego and were focused on that."[4] Shortly before his death, in a widely publicized letter to the Pope, Merton urged that not only contemplatives, but all people should "dare to penetrate your own silence" and "risk the sharing of that solitude with the lonely other who seeks God through you and with you," so that "you will truly recover the light and the capacity to understand what is beyond words and beyond explanations because it is too close to be explained: it is the intimate union in the depths of your own heart, of God's spirit and your own secret inmost self, so that you and He are in all truth One Spirit."[5]

Teilhard de Chardin says the loss of self (used as Jung would use *ego*) brings, "the irresistible rise, in the depth of my consciousness, of some sort of Other, more me than myself."[6] The British Bible scholar C. H. Dodd describes "the condition of inward harmony when all elements of the personality are organized about a single centre, and division and conflict are at an end."[7] The American Quaker Thomas R. Kelly describes the experience which Jung calls the Self encounter in these words:

> The sense of Presence is as if two beings were joined in one single configuration, and the center of gravity is not in us but in that Other. As two bodies, closely attached together and whirling in the air, are predominantly determined by the heavier body, so does the sense of Presence carry within it a sense of our lives being in large part guided, dynamically moved from beyond our usual selves. Instead of being the active, hurrying church worker and the anxious, careful planner of shrewd moves toward the good life, we become pliant creatures, less brittle, less obstinately rational. The energizing, dynamic center is not in us but in the Divine Presence in which we share.[8]

It should be clear from all these descriptions, Jungian and Christian, that the Self is, so to speak, larger and more than the ego. In fact, a major danger at the times of encounters with the Self is that the ego may become inflated by identifying with the Self, instead of realizing the Other to be the "heavier body" in the relationship.

Jungian studies of Self imagery are especially helpful, even to those familiar with similar experiences from their religious traditions, because of their identification of many of the patterns in which Self imagery appears. These observations can lead far beyond the traditional ideas of God-images, thus broadening the ability to recognize Self images. No matter how comprehensive a picture of God people have, their images are always less than God.

Self images always carry a great sense of power and authority for the dreamer. Coming as they do in crucial times for the dreamer, when basic attitudes and ways of life are at a turning point or crossroad, they carry numinous energy for the needed changes. Sometimes these Self images appear in dreams as people, but they carry a sense of wisdom, and the dreamer senses a larger-than-life importance in them. They may be specifically a religious person from the dreamer's own faith. For example, one way of speaking about the "gift" dream where Jesus came to take away the dreamer's husband from the hospital room (discussed at the end of chapter 14) would be to say that the dreamer encountered Jesus as a symbol of the Self. From that encounter, she was transformed from a fearful, anxious person into a strong and peaceful one. She knew her husband's death was "all right." The dream of Jesus (a primary Self image in our culture, as well as for the dreamer personally) reconciled her to the dreaded death of her loved one and gave meaning to her loss.

Even if the person is not a known figure, there is a God-like sense of power. Wallace's tribal dream in chapter 14 contains such a figure in the great-grandfather. His "authority surpassed all others," and he was thus able to save Wallace and reconcile the apparently irreconcilable opposites with which he was faced.

Sometimes such Self figures appear as huge or giant people, their size indicating their significance. One such figure of wisdom appeared only by his footprints in this dream of an Australian nun:

> A group of people were looking for a treasure hidden in the area. A man and I knew where it was hidden, but did not go to the spot.
>
> One day he and I returned from a boating trip on the ocean and climbed the steps of the cliff which led to the group of buildings in which we were staying. As we reached the top of the cliff, we saw large footprints on the ground. Each was drawn in white ochre. The actual shape of the foot had a double line; each had a cross on the ball of the foot; and each was numbered near the heel. They commenced with a circle and then went up beside the buildings and then round behind the chapel to the spot where the

treasure was. I knew that these footprints belonged to a giant Australian aborigine.

This is a complicated dream, which impressed the dreamer deeply. She described her personal associations with the aborigines as very moving to her. She thought them a beautiful, gentle people who had been mercilessly exploited and mistreated in their own land; she loved them very much and honored their myths and stories, their way of being and of relating to the land. She mourned their lives. The power they held for her as a symbol of deep wisdom was clear. To what treasure could the numbered footsteps of this giant aborigine be leading her.

In the first part of the dream, she had been boating on the ocean with an unknown animus figure; the collective unconscious had been traversed to get to this point. When she was asked about the "group of buildings," the other important set of associations appeared. She had recognized the chapel in the dream as being an actual chapel she knew, one with historical significance for her order in Australia—the Franklin Street Chapel. In this chapel, the foundress of her religious order, in a painful episode in church history, had been excommunicated by the bishop in what was essentially a power struggle over who would have the authority to make decisions about the order, the nuns themselves or the bishop. As can be imagined, this power struggle was deeply significant for the sisters in her order. Eventually, the foundress was reinstated but the memory, of course, remained.

Even in the midst of these significant symbols, one homely play on words is found in the dream. The steps lead around behind the chapel—to "see what was behind it all," as the saying goes. So somehow for the dreamer, this scene was a crucial one. It was important for her (in order to find her treasure) to find what lay behind all this—behind the historical events—and the exploited aborigine leads the way. With the changes in her church since Vatican II, it is not surprising that such questions need to be faced anew and understood by a religious sister. The issues of power in the order are raised, but the dream seems to suggest significance beyond the surface ones—issues about where *her* treasure lies, to be refleted upon in the full awareness of the history, both of the order and of the aborigines. The giant aborigine—a Self image—goes before her toward the hidden treasure. Such a dream remains a source of wisdom for the rest of the dreamer's life.

The wise old women and wise old men who come to us in dreams sometimes appear not so much huge or old as ageless, so that it is difficult to say whether they are very old or very young or both. Two women who carry the opposites of young and old appeared in this dream of a fifty-five-year-old woman:

> Two females—one holding a cement block—or the corner of a cement block—broken off from a sidewalk or from the base of a large statue. The women are trying to make an exchange. The older woman would like to have the cement block. The other person is much younger, more nearly a child, with long hair, wearing a white dress of flimsy material. I looked, hoping to see a wreath of flowers on her head, but I only imagined it because it would have looked appropriate.

The dreamer was extremely self-critical and full of anxiety. Her associations with these figures made them seem like Self images. She had a feeling of wanting to protect the younger woman, though she was "unafraid, virginal, innocent, and beautiful." She loved the older woman as well, but she added that the younger one, "though she was young, might have been a million years old. She was also ancient." Finally, after a long silence, the dreamer said, "She is *all* of me."

These figures seem to carry a larger possibility than the dreamer had heretofore recognized in herself. They seem like an inborn germ of her wholeness, as she finally manages to say, despite her self-deprecating habit of mind. Two months later, she dreamed:

> I saw an old woman. She was beautiful, snow-white hair—wavy, not curly.
> She was wearing a pale, dusty-rose gown or robe. It was almost mauve. She was sitting. Her face was infinitely kind.
> I walked up to her, and she looked at me without any censure. Her manner was total acceptance of me as I stood there in front of her.
> I said, "I can't make any promises." But she didn't alter her expression or her attitude.

The clarity of the Self image has increased in this dream; the "organ of acceptance" is viably experienced by the dreamer. She is obviously amazed by the sense of acceptance when she habitually expects censure from the world. Even in the face of the acceptance, she cannot promise anything, but the acceptance does not change. The dreamer has really encountered love that will not let her go. Such figures are described as "manna" personalities—people who give magical nourishment or nurture from an inexhaustible supply.

Another manner in which the Self manifests in dreams is in a disembodied voice, like the voice of God, which pronounces some statement to the dreamer. Such statements are usually brief, perhaps one sentence, sometimes with no visual image at all, but they carry a significance for the dreamer, as if they have received a direct "message." The voice may say something like, "What happens is preparation for the future" or "You don't know God forgives"—as happened in two actual dreams. No dream should be taken as absolute; the conscious point of view must always be maintained in order to "test the spirits," but such one-liners should be taken seriously.

The Self can also appear in dreams as a divine child. There are many divine child manifestations in history, mythology, and art—notably the Christ Child, whose coming excites more interest than any other holiday in the year—even with those who have no conscious faith connection with the Christian religion. The Self as a divine child seems to carry not only the power and authority of other Self figures, but to carry also the future, the possibility of a new beginning. The child comes out of the past, the tradition, and unites it with the possibility of a new future. Such figures seem to represent or personify the urge to realize oneself beyond the old limits.

In a dream which combined such imagery of the child, Christmas, and snake imagery, a parish priest dreamed:

> I go to the house of friends who are also members of my parish for a party. It is night. I walk through several rooms and arrive at a buffet with an abundance of food. The woman of the house kisses me on the cheek. I enter another room where the man of the house is sitting.
>
> I ask why the bare Christmas tree has not been decorated. He explains that only his daughter Mary is able to decorate the tree. Only she knows how to pick up the snakes to put on the tree. He calls her and she comes in and takes the snakes and freely tosses them on to the tree as decoration.

The dream seemed important to him, and it does bring together a number of transformation motifs. He described the couple as bright, highly spiritual, and competent. The woman was a type he described as an "earth mother." The little girl, Mary, he described as "lovely, spontaneous, a charmer, the sweetheart of the parish"; she was about four in the dream. Interestingly, this dream of a Christmas tree occurred in the middle of the summer—hardly a "day-remnant" dream!

A new awareness (the snakes, the feminine—both as earth mother and spontaneous child) come together to celebrate and to decorate the Christmas tree of new beginnings.

One of the most beautiful of such "divine child" dreams we have seen was a dream of his own reported by Thomas Merton:

> I am invited to a party. The people are dressed in fine new clothes walking about by the waterfront of a small fishing village of old stone houses. The gay, light dresses of the women contrast with the dark stones of the houses. I am invited to the party with them, and suddenly they are all gone, and the party is much farther away than I thought it would be. I must get there in a boat. I am all alone; the boat is at the quay.
>
> A man of the town says that for five dollars I can get across on a yacht. I have five dollars, more than five dollars, hundreds of dollars, and also francs. He takes me to the yacht, but it is not a yacht. It is a workaday fishing schooner, which I prefer. But it does not move; we try in many ways to make it move, and it seems to have moved a little. But then I know that I must strike out and swim.
>
> And I am swimming ahead in the beautiful magic water of the bay. From the clear depths of the water comes a wonderful life to which I am not entitled, a life and a power which I both love and fear. I know that by diving down into the water I can find wonders and joys, but that it is not for me to dive down; rather I must go to the other side, and I am indeed swimming to the other side. The other side is there. The end of the swim. The house is on the shore. The wide summer house which I am reaching with the strength that came to me from the water. The water is great and vast beneath me as I come toward the shore. And I have arrived. I am out of the water. I know now all that I must do in the summer house. I know that I must first play with this dog who comes running from one of the halls.
>
> I know the Child will come, and He comes. The Child comes and smiles. It is the smile of a Great One, hidden. He gives me, in simplicity, two pieces of buttered white bread, the ritual and hieratic meal given to all who come to stay.[9]

We have no opportunity to hear the personal associations of the dreamer, but the journal in which the dream is printed was first published in 1965, during the meetings of Vatican II. Merton made no secret of his enthusiasm for the reforms instituted in those years and subsequent to them, nor of his occasional impatience with the slow pace of some reform. It seems appropriate to connect this with the "workaday fishing schooner" in which he traveled, as a Trappist monk. His own leadership in exploring the depths of spiritual growth is beautifully evoked by the image of his swimming in the "magic water" from which the wonderful life comes, which he both loves and fears. The Child is the Self who reconciles in his being the tradition and the future, feeding Merton with the wholesome priestly communion given to all "who come to stay."

One of the helpful observations Jung made was the universal incidence of the number *four* in motifs of the process of individuation—there are four functions, four directions. Whenever the number four or some squared or quadrated form appears in a dream, Jung has noted that some aspect of the dreamer's wholeness is constellated. Furthermore, he noted that circles seem to represent wholeness in a natural level—that which is complete, without beginning or end. The squares seem to indicate wholeness possibilities on a more conscious level. Once one is sensitized to look for these symbols, it is quite remarkable how many can be observed, including a squared circle or an encircled square. Ezekiel's first vision in the Bible repeats these themes. Rose windows in cathedrals are examples, and Tibetan Buddhism has quadrated circles as objects of meditation. They are called *mandalas,* or magic circles, and Jungians refer to spontaneously produced squares, circles, or fourfold symbols as mandalas.

A related image of wholeness is a round stone, including also the philosopher's stone, precious stones or jewels (especially the hardest stone, the diamond), crystals, and the *lapis,* the alchemical symbol of God within. Stones seem to represent something permanent, which can be polished by great work or perfected by burning away the dross which mars its beauty. These materials may carry these suggestions in part because of their basic connection with nature—they are "givens"; they exist; they just *are.* Yet they can be worked on, in a manner that symbolically suggests the human growth process.

One woman had an interesting mandala dream near the beginning of her journey into the unconscious:

There was a difficult space rendezvous which was handled expertly. The astronauts got safely to earth. Then a sphere of some kind was to be retrieved from the spacecraft, but in transferring it to a ship, it slipped into the ocean. It was a real disappointment that, after all the difficult maneuvers were done so successfully, an easier task at the end was goofed up.

Her work began because of a series of frightening dreams, dreams which seemed to contain life-threatening images. At the same time, she received a tentative diagnosis of a life-threatening disease from her doctor. She had weathered this "difficult maneuver" with the discovery of a misdiagnosis, but now the dream suggests, she is in danger of letting her wholeness slip back into the collective unconscious when the immediate danger seems past.

She decided to stay with her personal journey, and her work later culminated in a re-integration of a strong contemplative side which had been left behind years before in the dreamer's active life of social work. She found that she could reclaim the lost contemplative side of herself without losing her social conscience and service.

Mandala patterns in circles or squares can be quite simple and still indicate that something involving the dreamer's wholeness is involved— some ordering principle. In the first year we studied in Zurich, Jean had such a dream:

I decided to put the Thanksgiving turkey on a large platter. There was a sliced pineapple on top of it. At a crossing of two sidewalks, I said, "Wallace loves pineapple, and he thinks almost everything is better with some pineapple." Then I thought how odd it was how much Wallace likes pineapple and how much my father hates it.

Jean gave the analyst a description of the customary family celebration of our national holiday, though she said she had never heard of anyone putting sliced pineapple on the turkey. He asked her to draw a diagram of where she was standing, and when she drew a cross with herself in the middle, he said, "I thought so," and pointed out that this was a simple mandala pattern. Therefore, something concerned with Jean's wholeness would be suggested in the dream imagery.

It was factually true that Jean's father disliked pineapple and that Wallace liked it very much. When asked, Jean said that she liked pineapple, too. The analyst then suggested that she turn her attention to her current life to get the situation to which the dream probably referred. He said there was some attitude or decision, probably connected with the family, where Jean's wholeness involved choosing a way that was like Wallace, rather than a way that was like her father. The dream gave her the clue to recognize the significance of the particular attitude she must come to terms with.

After a year of analysis, Jean had another mandala dream, this one much more numinous:

> I was on the land of my parents' place, and there was an old shed there with water under it. I looked in the water and saw a rope. I began to pull the rope up out of the water and continued to pull for a time until a chain came up. Then I pulled the chain for a long time, until finally some wood appeared at the end of it. I pulled and pulled on it until finally I had pulled all of it up and could tell that it was an old mill wheel that had been in the deep water—so deep, no one remembered it was there. I was so excited. Then, I began to see how these stepping-stones of the walk to the shed had been part of the mill. I began to bring all the rocks up to the wheel, carrying them toward the wheel to put it all together again. Some had to be dug up; some were very large. All of it was hard work, or should have been, but it seemed all joy to me.

This remarkable dream is complex, but some of the themes are quite clear to anyone sensitized to symbolic language. The dream had the quality of mystery and power which accompanies Self dreams, and the round circle of the mill wheel suggests the natural wholeness deep in the water—"so deep, no one remembered it was there." Jean's sense of excitement accords with such a discovery. She had been hard at work, pulling up from the unconscious many connected strands of her life before the mill wheel appeared.

The placing of the stepping-stones "to put it all together again" suggests the beginning stages of an integration of her wholeness, and there is encouragement for this task, despite how hard the work is, in the joy she experiences in the dream as she works.

The analyst supplied some general amplification which enriched the understanding of the dream even more. She said the miller was a kind of trickster because he was the first person who harnessed nature to do his work—grinding food by the action of river water to turn the mill wheel. This is like stealing fire from the gods—a trick on nature in the process of civilization. So it became clear that Jean needed to be more in touch with the deep natural wholeness within her—not so "heady" as to be shut away from her innate folk wisdom and wholeness. In this manner, she could put together the "stepping-stones" of her life.

This instinctual, natural connectedness of the Self may also be represented by animals—like the helpful animals in myths and fairy tales, who so frequently help the hero to complete the task safely. One such Self image appeared in the dream of a woman we will call Ellen:

> I'm in a house in a wooded area with other people. One of the guys does something to attract some animals outside. Soon a couple of reindeer climb down the clifflike rocks behind the house. Then one reindeer tries to open the back kitchen window, which opens out at the top. As I push against the window to keep it shut, the deer becomes a young male god, and the window a glass door. The god is stronger than me, but leaves after proving he could come in if he wanted to. I believe he'll be back, so with someone's help, I triple lock and bolt the door.
>
> A storm is coming and the other young people run to the door for shelter. I motion to them to go to the side door, which shuts easily. As I let them in, I ask for two volunteers—one to stand at the bolted door and motion people to the side door, and one to let them in the side door. The house is now a co-ed college residence. I ask the side-door volunteer, "We're only letting our own people in, right?" wanting to keep the god out. But she answered, "I'm not going to cripple anyone."

At her initial attempts to understand the dream, Ellen could see several clear motifs presented. She was obviously trying to avoid this powerful reindeer god, whose courtesy evidently inspires him to leave until she is more ready for him. She is still frightened, and even though faced with a "storm" in her life, she goes to a great deal of trouble to try to make sure he cannot enter if he returns. A shadow figure is not so sure as Ellen that he should be kept out, with the suggestion that someone (Ellen?) might be "crippled" by keeping the god out.

Yet the major mystery remained: what was a reindeer god and what could it signify? She had never heard of such a creature and did not know if any mythology about it existed. Yet the dream impressed her so that she decided to look for some general amplification of this symbol—especially since it seemed to be a Self image. She began with an encyclopedia article about reindeer, where she found some symbolically suggestive material.

Reindeer are strong, fast swimmers who cannot sink because their coat holds in air pockets. Ellen was encouraged by this because she felt it was safe for her to "swim" in the waters of the unconscious. They are timid, easily frightened and cling together; when they get excited, they mill around in large circles. Again she identified with these facts—she saw herself as easily frightened and inclined to "go around in circles in my head" when something is not resolved. They have a fast, swinging trot that can be kept up indefinitely; Ellen liked the suggestion of perseverance, of steadily sticking to one's own path. They existed a million years ago and are about the same today as then, which gave her a sense of continuity and universality. They can pull heavy loads, and only children can ride them.

At a later time, making a retreat at a monastery, Ellen found time to search in another library, and this time she found the reindeer myths from Siberia and Scandinavia. In this mythology, the reindeer escort the dead to the underworld. The reindeer carries the person who has just died safely by avoiding and going around the dangerous places—so a reindeer was placed in the grave at burial.

She also found that the soul of the shaman takes the shape of a reindeer bull. As the religious leader, the shaman offers sacrifice, has to keep his body healthy, and has great endurance and protection from bodily harm.

Ellen reacted to this reindeer myth with fear. She was somewhat comforted by the idea of having a "reindeer god" to carry her safely around danger points in her "death-to-self journey," as she called her spiritual journey, but it also felt scary to her. The numinous experience always contains the mixture of longing and fear, as we have said.

The shaman idea scared her even more. She did not want to be a religious leader or healer. However, she prayed that she could let herself be a child and accept whatever change or death in herself God might ask of her. The next day she tried to "dialogue" with the reindeer god and felt a sense of reassurance of its protection, but she also knew that she needed to remember that only the child and those who have "died" can ride the reindeer—though she had no idea why. Then she had another reindeer dream:

> The reindeer is standing at a lake and looking down into the lake. There is a beam from each of his eyes to the water. I say, "His eyes are liquid beams."

The next day she went into the mountains near the monastery and put herself into the prayer she calls "just being in God's presence." Suddenly, she found herself imaginatively riding the reindeer and felt as if she were a child. After a time the rhythm of the ride changed to fury, and she felt again the tantrums of her early childhood. Another day, again in her favorite spot on the mountain, she re-experienced her struggle to be born.

Ellen's mother had a difficult labor, which lasted fourteen hours when Ellen was being born. Her mother was paralyzed with pain because of the pressure on a particular nerve and so could not push the baby out. Ellen was born with a badly misshapen head from the pressure of the birth.

From these remarkable experiences in prayer and active imagination, as well as later work on this theme, Ellen came to understand that the rages she felt from time to time were connected with her own struggle to be born as a baby. The feeling was just the same. She realized that when she feels that kind of anger, she can feel the pressure on her like the birth canal, as if everything is pushing against her, not letting her "live."

Ellen later discovered that when these angers come upon her, she can imaginatively ride her reindeer god (like a child). Something about the steady, strong rhythmic pace of a reindeer god is strengthening and calming for her. She quite literally is aided by this deep, natural Self image when she invites him in to help her. This is the kind of "regression" into old pains and sorrows which the Jungians would understand as a regression in the service of the Self—of the enlarging and maturing of the personality.

This account of the reindeer dreams of Ellen and the research that she engaged in, together with the active imagination and insight which followed, is a living example of the mysterious archetypal possibilities in dreams. Yet this report only skims the surface of the complexity and interaction of the inner and outer meaning of this symbol for Ellen. Such experiences have come to people from preliterate times (as evidenced by remnants of art and artifacts), and they continue unabated in modern urban people such as Ellen. Connecting to the individual significance of such experiences is one way of connecting to the spiritual or mystical meaning beyond the personal.

In whatever symbols of transformation the psyche offers, this kind of attention and honoring, listening and exploring the images, even if faithfully followed will not necessarily make a spiritual experience or a transformation happen. They cannot be forced. One can, however, as Jung suggests, draw near the experience and wait upon it—there to encounter the symbolic inner treasures that can lead to personal transformation.

Joseph Campbell has demonstrated that all the world's creation myths, including the contemporary biological view, have a common image of original oneness: "the unfolding through time of all things from one."[10] By recognizing the inner mystery of this image, Campbell says, "every god that is dead can be conjured to life again." Creation and growth arise from the interplay of this oneness with the conscious awareness of the individual which breaks apart from the oneness and returns consciously into relation with the oneness. This is the profound and continuing movement of human transformation.

Notes

Jung, *Collected Works—The Collected Works of C.G. Jung,* trans. R.F.C. Hull, 20 vols., Bollingen Series XX (Princeton: Princeton University Press, 1953–1979).

Chapter 1. Dreams
1. Gladys A. Reichard, *Navaho Religion* (2d ed., in one volume, Bollingen Series XVIII; Princeton, N.J.: Princeton University Press, 1970), pp. 550–51.
2. Mircea Eliade, *Shamanism,* trans. Willard R. Trask (Bollingen Series LXXVI; New York, N.Y.: Bollingen Foundation, 1964), p. 103.
3. John G. Neihardt, *Black Elk Speaks* (Morrow edition, 1932; New York, N.Y.: Pocket Books, 1972).
4. C. Kerényi, *Eleusis,* trans. Ralph Manheim (Bollingen Series LXV 4; New York, N.Y.: Bollingen Foundation, 1967), p. 83.
5. C. Kerényi, *Asklepios,* trans. Ralph Manheim (Bollingen Series LXV 3; New York, N.Y.: Bollingen Foundation, 1959), p. 34.
6. C. Kerényi, *Zeus and Hera,* trans. Christopher Holme (Bollingen Series LXV 5; Princeton N.J.: Princeton University Press, 1975), pp. 91–92.
7. Jung, *Collected Works,* VIII, par. 683.

Chapter 2. The Unconscious
1. Jung, *Collected Works,* XVIII, par. 1156.
2. Jung, *Collected Works,* III, par. 390.
3. Ibid., par. 565.
4. Jung, *Collected Works,* XIII, par. 11.
5. Jung, *Collected Works,* XVIII, par. 84.
6. Ibid., par. 1156.
7. Jung, *Collected Works,* IX (I), par. 91.
8. Ibid., par. 155.
9. Jung, *Collected Works,* III, par. 566.
10. Jung, *Collected Works,* V, par. 450.
11. Jung, *Collected Works,* XVIII, par. 596.
12. Jung, *Collected Works,* V, par. 344.

Chapter 3. Symbolic Language
1. Jung, *Collected Works,* V, par. 114.
2. Jung, *Collected Works,* XVIII, par. 482.

3. Jung, *Collected Works*, IX (I), par. 80.
4. Jung, *Collected Works, XIII, par. 397.*

Chapter 4. Approaching the Dream

1. Jung, *Collected Works*, XVIII, par. 248.
2. C.G. Jung, *Memories, Dreams, Reflections*, recorded and edited by Aniela Jaffe, trans. Richard and Clara Winston (New York, N.Y.: Vintage Books, 1961), p. 133.
3. Jung, *Collected Works*, VIII, par. 230.
4. Ibid.
5. Jung, *Collected Works*, XVIII, par. 181.
6. Jung, *Collected Works*, VII, par. 130.
7. Jung, *Collected Works*, XVIII, par. 522.

Chapter 7. Transformation

1. Erik H. Erikson, *Childhood and Society* (New York, N.Y.: W. W. Norton & Company, Inc., 1950; 2nd ed., 1963), pp. 247–274.
2. Gordon W. Allport, *Letters from Jenny* (New York, N.Y.: Harcourt Brace & World, Inc., 1965), pp. 157–58.
3. Marie-Louise von Franz, *Patterns of Creativity Mirrored in Creation Myths* (Zurich, Switzerland: Spring Publications, 1972), p. 13
4. Edward C. Whitmont, *The Symbolic Quest* (New York: G. P. Putnam's Sons for the C.G. Jung Foundation for Analytical Psychology, 1969), p. 296.
5. James A. Hall, *Clinical Use of Dreams* (New York: Grune & Stratton, subsidiary of Harcourt Brace Jovanovich, 1977), pp. 147–48.
6. Jung, *Collected Works*, IX (I), par. 80.

Chapter 9. Shadow

1. Jung, *Collected Works*, VII, p. 66, n. 5.
2. Carl G. Jung and M.-L. von Franz, ed., *Man and His Symbols* (Garden City, N.Y.: Doubleday & Company, Inc., 1964), pp. 170–176.
3. Galway Kinnell, "St. Francis and the Sow," in *Mortal Acts, Mortal Words* (Boston: Houghton Mifflin Co., 1980), p. 9.

Chapter 10. Anima

1. Jung, *Collected Works*, VII, par. 296.
2. Jung, *Collected Works*, XVII, par. 338.
3. Jung, *Collected Works*, VI, par. 376.
4. Jung and von Franz, *Man and His Symbols*, p. 188.
5. Jung, *Collected Works*, XII, par. 65.
6. Jung, *Collected Works*, IX (I), par. 147.
7. Jung, *Collected Works*, XIII, par. 216
8. Jung, *Collected Works*, XVIII, par. 352.
9. Jung, *Collected Works*, VIII, par. 507.

Chapter 11. Animus

1. Jane Hollister Wheelwright, in collaboration with Eleanor Haas, Barbara McClintock, and Audrey Blodgett, *The Death of a Woman* (New York: St. Martin's Press, 1981), p. 278.

Chapter 12. Snakes

1. Jung, *Collected Works,* IX (I), par. 282.
2. Jung, *Collected Works,* XIII, par. 184.
3. C. Kerényi, *Asklepios,* p. 36.
4. Quoted in ibid. pp. 13–14.
5. Edward C. Whitmont, *Return of the Goddess* (New York: Crossroad, 1982), pp. 249–50.
6. C. Kerényi, *Dionysos,* trans. Ralph Manheim (Bollingen Series LXV 2; Princeton, N.J.: Princeton University Press, 1976), pp. 61–64.

Chapter 13. Trickster

1. Jung, *Collected Works,* IX (I), par. 465.
2. Ibid., par. 478.
3. Ibid., par. 480.
4. Jung and von Franz, *Man and His Symbols,* pp. 149–51.
5. C.L. Barber, *Shakespeare's Festive Comedy: A Study of Dramatic Form and its Relation to Social Custom* (Princeton, N.J.: Princeton University Press, 1959), pp. 4–7.
6. G.K. Chesterton, *St. Francis of Assisi* (Garden City, N.Y.: Doubleday & Company, Inc., 1924; Image Books 1957), p. 83
7. Ibid., p. 120.
8. Jung, *Collected Works,* VII, pars. 111, 112.
9. Jung, *Collected Works,* IX (I), par. 82.
10. Jung, *Collected Works,* XIII, par. 294.

Chapter 14. Death and Rebirth

1. M. Scott Peck, *The Road Less Traveled* (New York: Simon and Schuster, 1978), p. 193.

Chapter 16. The Self

1. Jung and von Franz, *Man and His Symbols,* p. 162.
2. Jung, *Collected Works,* XI, par. 758.
3. Jung, *Collected Works,* XIV, par. 284.
4. Monica Furlong, *Merton: A Biography* (New York: Harper & Row, Publishers, Inc.; Bantam Books, 1981), p. xix.
5. Quoted in Henri J.M. Nouwen, *Pray to Live: Thomas Merton: A Contemplative Critic* (Notre Dame, Indiana: Fides Publishers, Inc., 1972), p. 41.
6. William Johnston, *The Still Point: Reflections on Zen and Christian Mysticism* (New York: Fordham University Press, 1970), p. 168.
7. C.H. Dodd, *The Epistle of Paul to the Romans* (London: Hodder & Stoughton, 1932; Collins, Fontana Books, 1959), p. 138.
8. Thomas R. Kelly, *A Testament of Devotion* (New York: Harper & Brothers, Publishers, 1941), p. 96.
9. Thomas Merton, *Conjectures of a Guilty Bystander* (Garden City, N.Y.: Doubleday & Company, Inc., 1965; Image Books, 1968) pp. 29–30.
10. Joseph Campbell, *The Way of the Animal Powers* (San Francisco: Harper & Row, 1983), p. 10.

Selected Readings on Jung

Jung's writings fill twenty volumes of the *Collected Works*. In addition, useful insights can be found in his autobiography, *Memories, Dreams, Reflections,* and in the published volumes of his *Letters.*

There are several books on Jungian dream interpretation. Three which we have used in teaching are:

John A. Sanford, *Dreams and Healing* (New York: Paulist Press, 1978), a brief survey of theory in nontechnical language, followed by two dream series with interpretation.

James A. Hall, *Jungian Dream Interpretation* (Toronto: Inner City Books, 1983), a useful handbook of theory and practice by a psychiatrist–Jungian analyst.

Mary Ann Mattoon, *Applied Dream Analysis* (Washington, D.C.: V. H. Winston & Sons, 1978), an organized collection of Jung's writings about dreams.

Man and His Symbols (New York: Dell, 1964) contains the last major essay Jung wrote, designed to introduce his thought to the average lay reader. Also highly recommended for interpretation is Part 3 by Marie-Louise von Franz, "The Process of Individuation."

Those interested in *Jung and Christianity* will benefit from Wallace B. Clift's book of that name (New York: Crossroad, 1982), as well as the books of Morton Kelsey and John A. Sanford.

Extremely helpful on the anima-animus is Sanford's *The Invisible Partners* (New York: Paulist Press, 1980).

The best introductory surveys of Jung's thought are: Jolande Jacobi, *The Psychology of C. G. Jung* (New Haven: Yale University Press, 7th ed., 1968), and Edward Whitmont, *The Symbolic Quest* (New York: G.P. Putnam's Sons, 1969).

Among many excellent books on the changing understanding of women are two of Ann Belford Ulanov's books: *The Feminine in Jungian Psychology and in Christian Theology* (Evanston: Northwestern University Press, 1971) and *Receiving Woman* (Philadelphia: The Westminster Press, 1981).

A fine description of the practice of Jung's psychology is June Singer's *Boundaries of the Soul* (Garden City, N.Y.: Doubleday & Company, Inc., 1972).

Then, as John Donne might say, "When thou hast done, thou hast not done," for there are more—many more—excellent and helpful books on Jung.

Index

"Love Song of J. Alfred Prufrock" (Eliot), 41–42

magic, 3
malnutrition in dreams, 112
mandalas, 141–43
marriage motif in dreams, 80, 130
Memories, Dreams, Reflections (Jung), 117
men as animus figures in dreams, 80–85, 87, 137
Merton, Thomas, 134–35, 14–41
metaphor, 30–33
mother persona figure, 56, 57

narrative, 36–38
neuroses, 49
Neutze, Diana, 99
nightmares, 126
nuns, dreams of, 84, 136–37

objective correlative in poetry, 41
objective and subjective dreams, 23–24
organ of acceptance, 138

Peck, M. Scott, 108
Perry, John Weir, 14
personal unconcious, 11, 22
personification, 33–34
pigs, 67–69
premonition in dreams, 117–18, 136
primitive cultures, myths and magic of, 3, 4, 144–45, 147
projections, 63, 67, 77–78
puns in dreams, 34

reality, 3–6, 15
regression, 28
religion, 4, 51–52, 67, 84
    dreams about, 84, 129–31, 139, 140
    growth and, 147

self and, 133–37, 139, 141
snakes and, 90–92
tricksters and, 102–3, 105–6
Rime of the Ancient Mariner, The (Coleridge), 99
Road Less Traveled, The (Peck), 108
Roots of Renewal in Myths and Madness (Perry), 14–15

sacrifice, 51–52
"Saint Francis and the Sow" (Kinnel), 67–68
Sandford, John A., 5, 25
Saturnalia festival, 103
Seegar, Pete, 17
sexuality, 7, 9–11, 64–66, 80–81, 131–32
shamans, 4, 145
Swiss watchmaker in dreams, 39–40
symbolic language, 14, 143
symbols, 6–7, 15–19, 25–26, 96, 97
    eggs as, 93
    snakes as, 90–91

teeth, loss of, dreams about, 127–28
Tennyson, Alfred Lord, 33
Thomas Aquinas, Saint, 5
Tillich, Paul, 15
"To his Coy Mistress" (Marvell), 35

unconscious, the, 6–7, 9–11, 20, 25, 47–48, 60, 78
urinating black man, dream about, 97–99

Vatican II, 137, 141
Victorian stereotype, shadow of, 64–66

waking up, dreams of, 125–26
weapons in dreams, 85–86
Whitmont, Edward, 91
women as anima figures in dreams, 72–73, 75–77